FITZGERALD'S
THE GREAT GATSBY

CONTINUUM READER'S GUIDES

Achebe's Things Fall Apart – Ode Ogede

William Blake's Poetry – Jonathan Roberts

Conrad's Heart of Darkness – Allan Simmons

Dickens's Great Expectations – Ian Brinton

Sylvia Plath's Poetry – Linda Wagner-Martin

FITZGERALD'S
THE GREAT GATSBY

A Reader's Guide

NICOLAS TREDELL

continuum

CONTINUUM International Publishing Group
The Tower Building
11 York Road
London
SE1 7NX

80 Maiden Lane
Suite 704
New York
NY 10038

First published 2007

British Library Cataloguing-in-Publication Data
A catalogue record for this book is available from the British Library.

ISBN – 10: 0 8264 9010 7 (hardback)
           0 8264 9011 5 (paperback)
ISBN – 13: 978 08264 9010 0 (hardback)
           978 08264 9011 7 (paperback)

Library of Congress Cataloging-in-Publication Data
A catalog record for this book is available from the Library of Congress.

Typeset by Servis Filmsetting Ltd, Manchester
Printed and bound in Great Britain by
MPG Books Ltd, Bodmin, Cornwall

CONTENTS

NOTE

Gatsby page references are to the 2000 Penguin Classics paperback.

Crack-Up references are to the 1962 New Directions paperback.

Definitions are from the 11th edition of the *Concise Oxford English Dictionary*, unless otherwise stated.

CHAPTER 1

CONTEXTS

FITZGERALD'S LIFE

Scott Fitzgerald was a legend in his own lifetime and has become even more so since his death. He seems to epitomize an American era – the 'Jazz Age' of the 1920s – and to symbolize its delights, dangers and defeats. His spectacular early success as a writer, his frantic pursuit of pleasure, his fraught relationship with his wife Zelda, and his decline into alcoholism, obscurity and premature death represents the trajectory of a generation. While his fiction is never simply autobiographical, his life and work are intricately interwoven and he created, in *The Great Gatsby*, one of the most pervasive and appealing of modern American myths.

Francis Scott Key Fitzgerald was born in St Paul, Minnesota, on 24 September 1896; his forenames were taken from his great-great-uncle, Francis Scott Key (1779–1843), who, in 1814, had written the song that would eventually be adopted as the American national anthem in 1931, 'The Star-Spangled Banner'. Fitzgerald's birth was haunted by death: three months earlier, two of his infant sisters had died. In 'Author's House' (1936), he identifies this loss as the point at which he started to be a writer. Another sister, born in 1900, lived just an hour; his only surviving sibling, Annabel, arrived in 1901.

The dominant theme of his boyhood, which would also figure strongly in his fiction, was social insecurity. He later wrote that he 'developed a two-cylinder inferiority complex' because of the division between the dual strands of his family background: an

1

Irish strand with the money, and an old American strand with 'the usual exaggerated ancestral pretensions' and the 'series of reticences and obligations that go under the poor old shattered word "breeding"'. The disparity between money and 'breeding' would be one of the key concerns of *Gatsby*.

Fitzgerald's sense of inferiority was increased by his father's downward mobility. When the novelist was born, Edward Fitzgerald owned a furniture factory, the American Rattan and Willow Works; but this failed less than two years later, in April 1898, and forced him to take a job as a wholesale grocery salesman with Proctor and Gamble in Buffalo, New York State. Then in July 1908, when Fitzgerald was 11, his father, then aged 55, lost his job; his son later saw this a decisive blow: 'That morning he had gone out a comparatively young man, a man full of strength, full of confidence. He came home that evening, an old man, a completely broken man.' His father had suffered an experience that would permeate his son's fiction: failure. The family moved back to St Paul; they were now dependent on the income from the mother's capital and while this allowed them to maintain a comfortable upper-middle-class lifestyle, it also highlighted, for Fitzgerald, the gap between his own, broken father and the successful men who lived around them in the Summit Avenue area of St Paul. The most famous of these was James J. Hill (1838–1916), the tycoon who had pushed the railroad across the West to the Pacific Coast. In *Gatsby*, Henry C. Gatz, the failed father, says that his son, if he had lived, would have been a great man like James J. Hill who would have helped to build up the country (p. 160).

Fitzgerald became a pupil at the St Paul Academy in September 1908 and first appeared in print the following year, at the age of 13, with a detective story, 'The Mystery of the Raymond Mortgage', in the school magazine. But his academic work was weak, and his family, hoping to improve it, sent him, in 1911, to Newman School, a Catholic boarding school in Hackensack, New Jersey. His academic work did not improve much there and he was no great social success, but the stories he published in the Newman school magazine showed that he was developing an individual style and tone. His most important experience at Newman, however, was his friendship with Father Cyril Sigourney Webster Fay, an impressive, urbane priest with many interests. Fitzgerald would use him as the model for Monsignor Darcy in his first novel, *This Side of Paradise* (1920).

In September 1913, Fitzgerald went east to Princeton University, though his poor performance in the entrance exams had nearly denied him admission. He was disappointed at being, as he later put it in 'The Crack-Up' (1936), 'not big enough (or good enough) to play football' (p. 70), but he formed two friendships with fellow students that were to be important for his literary development. One was with John Peale Bishop (1892–1944), who taught him a great deal about poetry and who would later become a poet, essayist and novelist; the other and more lasting friendship was with Edmund Wilson (1895–1972), who would become one of America's leading literary critics, and, by Fitzgerald's own account in 'The Crack-Up', his 'intellectual conscience' (p. 79). Fitzgerald read widely, and contributed to the *Princeton Tiger*, the *Nassau Lit.* and to scripts for the Triangle Club shows, but his academic performance remained poor and forced him to withdraw from Princeton in December 1915. He returned to Princeton in September 1916 but never completed his degree.

Since Christmas 1914, Fitzgerald had maintained a romantic attachment to Ginevra King, a girl from St Paul who seemed to embody all his aspirations: she was beautiful and wealthy, held a high place in the social hierarchy, and had many admirers. But the relationship did not endure and came to an end in January 1917; it seemed to Fitzgerald to demonstrate his sense of the social and financial barrier which stopped poor boys from marrying rich girls – a concern that would be crucial to *Gatsby*.

On 6 April 1917, the USA entered the First World War, and Fitzgerald signed up for the army in May. He was commissioned as an infantry second lieutenant and in November he reported for duty to Fort Leavenworth in Kansas. It was there that he began the first draft of a semi-autobiographical novel, 'The Romantic Egotist'. He completed it in March 1918, while on leave from the army at Princeton, and submitted it to Scribner's. Three months later, in July 1918, he met Zelda Sayre, the daughter of a local judge, at a country club dance in Montgomery in Alabama, and fell for her. Scribner's returned 'The Romantic Egotist' in August 1918, with a letter suggesting revisions, probably written by Maxwell Perkins (1884–1947), an editor at Scribner's who would become very important to Fitzgerald and to *Gatsby*. Fitzgerald quickly tried to alter the novel to take account of these suggestions and sent it to Scribner's again, only to have it rejected once more.

In November 1918, Fitzgerald reported to Camp Mills, Long Island, to await embarkation for military service in Europe; but the war came to an end before his unit could be sent abroad. He would always regret that, as the title of a 1936 short story put it, 'I didn't get over'. In *Gatsby* he would portray, in the narrator, Nick Carraway, and in the eponymous hero, men who did get over and whose war service forms one of the bonds between them.

Fitzgerald returned to civilian life wanting to marry Zelda; but she would not rush into a marriage with a jobless, unproven writer. He got a job in New York writing copy for the Barron Collier advertising agency, and his rhyming slogan for a laundry in Muscatine, Iowa – 'We Keep You Clean in Muscatine' – made his boss feel that he had a future in the advertising business. Fitzgerald's experience of the advertising industry may have contributed to the strong awareness he shows in *Gatsby* of its power to provide iconic images and shape behaviour and desire, but his future lay elsewhere, and in the evenings he tried to pursue it, writing stories, sketches, film scripts, verses and jokes which he hoped would bring him recognition and money. He received many rejection slips, creating a frieze of 122 of them in his room, and sold only one story, 'Babes in the Wood' to the magazine *The Smart Set*, which paid him $30. This was hardly enough to convince Zelda to accept him as a prospective husband; in June 1919, she broke off their engagement.

It was time for decisive action; and in July 1919, Fitzgerald took a big gamble, threw up his job with Barron Collier and went back to live with his parents in St Paul and to rewrite 'The Romantic Egotist'. The gamble paid off: Maxwell Perkins of Scribner's accepted the revised version – now called *This Side of*

Paradise – in September 1919. While waiting for the novel to appear, Fitzgerald also started to get more short stories published and in February 1920 broke into the mass-circulation magazine market for the first time, with the publication of 'Head and Shoulders' in *The Saturday Evening Post* for a fee of $500; the *Post* would become his primary short-story market. It paid well and had a comparatively large circulation which reached 2,750,000 copies a week in the 1920s. In *Gatsby*, the *Post* is the magazine from which Jordan Baker reads aloud to Tom Buchanan (p. 22).

Fitzgerald was proving that he could earn enough money to support Zelda in the style to which she was accustomed. He began to visit her again in Montgomery and in January 1920 they became engaged once more. *This Side of Paradise* was published on 26 March 1920 and was an instant success. It is a lively and entertaining novel which uses a rich range of techniques to portray Amory Blaine's life from boyhood to young manhood. Its subject matter caught the mood of the moment, pleasing the young and shocking their elders because it showed privileged young people behaving with what was, at the time, unaccustomed freedom. The first print run of 3,000 copies sold out in three days.

Fitzgerald's triumph with *This Side of Paradise* enabled him to make Zelda his wife: they were married in New York on 3 April 1920 and honeymooned at the Biltmore. It confirmed the feeling which Fitzgerald, would later in 'The Crack-Up', attribute to his youthful self: 'Life was something you dominated if you were any good' (p. 69). He did not forget, however, what might have happened if he had not won the means to marry Zelda: 'The man with the jingle of money in his pocket who married [her] would always cherish an abiding distrust, an animosity, toward the leisure class – not the conviction of a revolutionary but the smouldering hatred of a peasant. In the years since then I have never been able to stop wondering where my friends' money came from, nor to stop thinking that at one time a sort of *droit de seigneur* [lord's right] might have been exercised to give one of them my girl' (p. 77). *Gatsby* focuses on a man with nothing in his pockets who loses a girl from the leisure class and then finds, when his pockets are full to overflowing, that it is too late to win her back; the phrase that Fitzgerald uses in 'The Crack-Up' – the 'jingle of money' – echoes Nick Carraway's words when he confirms Gatsby's observation that Daisy's voice is 'full of money': 'that was . . . the jingle of it' (p. 115).

After their marriage, Scott and Zelda plunged into the pursuit of pleasure and into the maelstrom of modern publicity, partying, leaping into fountains, riding on the roofs of taxicabs, giving interviews, constructing a vivid public identity for themselves. To finance this wild and luxurious lifestyle, Fitzgerald had to keep writing for magazines and, despite the excellence of some of his short fiction, a troubling split developed, in his own mind, and in the perception of his peers, between the stories that he wrote for money and the novels that he wrote to try to realize the ambition he had expressed to Edmund Wilson at Princeton: to be one of the greatest writers that ever lived. His first short-story collection, *Flappers and Philosophers*, came out in September 1920. In May to July 1921, the Fitzgeralds made their first trip to Europe and came back to St Paul for the birth of their first and only child, Scottie, on 26 October 1921. As Zelda came out of the anaesthetic, she said of her newborn daughter, 'I hope it's beautiful and a fool – a beautiful little fool' – words which Fitzgerald would later weave into Daisy's account, in *Gatsby*, of her remarks after the birth of her baby (p. 22).

Fitzgerald's second novel, *The Beautiful and Damned*, appeared on 4 March 1922. Longer and more sombre than *This Side of Paradise*, it followed the chaotic trail of a wannabe writer who waits for a large legacy to fall into his hands while his life and marriage disintegrate. It got fairly good reviews and sold quite well, but it was insufficiently accomplished to establish Fitzgerald as a major novelist, and did not make enough money to enable him to give up writing for magazines.

Fitzgerald seems to have begun to think about his third novel in June 1922, when he and Zelda were staying at the Yacht Club at White Bear Lake in Minnesota; he wrote to Maxwell Perkins that this novel would be set in the Midwest and New York in 1885 and would cover a shorter span of time than his two previous novels. He wanted it to be different from, and better than, its predecessors: as he told Perkins in a letter of July 1922, in a statement of intent which seems to anticipate his achievement in *Gatsby*: 'I want to write something *new* – something extraordinary and beautiful and simple + intricately patterned.'

In August 1922, the Fitzgeralds were asked to leave the Yacht Club because of their wild parties, and the following month, before they moved back east, Fitzgerald wrote the first of the *Gatsby* group of stories – the three short stories which appeared during the gestation of *Gatsby* and which seem related to the novel. The first, 'Winter Dreams' (1922), follows the passion of Dexter Green for Judy Jones from its awakening in his early adolescence, through their tortuous relationship when he is a young, rising entrepreneur, to his disillusionment when he learns that she is a married mother who has lost her looks and whose husband is drunk and unfaithful: the description of Dexter's response to Judy Jones's house was later removed from the magazine version of the story to become Jay Gatsby's reaction to Daisy's Louisville dwelling. The second story, '"The Sensible Thing"' (1924) is also about the loss of a dream; George O'Kelly is initially rejected by the girl he loves, Jonquil O'Cary, because he has neither job nor money, but when he makes good and returns to marry her, he realizes that the freshness of their first love can never be recaptured. The third story of the *Gatsby* group, 'Absolution' (1924), which Fitzgerald himself said was taken from the initial drafts of his third novel, has a Catholic element that is absent from *Gatsby* but the character of Rudolph Miller resembles the young Gatsby in his proneness to exalted fantasies and his rejection of a father who, like Henry C. Gatz, beats his son and admires James J. Hill.

In October 1922, the Fitzgeralds rented a house at Great Neck, Long Island, and it was this locale that provided the basis for the setting of *Gatsby*: Great Neck was favoured as a place of residence by nouveau riche show-business people while the inhabitants of Manhasset Neck, across the bay, were from families that had made their millions in the nineteenth century. In *Gatsby*, Great Neck and Manhasset Neck become West and East Egg. Fitzgerald's satirical play *The Vegetable* flopped in November 1923, and in April 1924, Scott and Zelda set off for France once more. Fitzgerald wrote *Gatsby* on the French Riviera in the summer and autumn of 1924 and sent it to Scribner's; Maxwell Perkins responded with two letters praising the novel but also making some criticisms. Fitzgerald revised the novel extensively on the galley proofs, and the final version was published on 10 April 1925.

Although the reviews of *Gatsby* were mixed and its sales sluggish, Fitzgerald would later regard the novel as the peak of his career which had shown him the road he should have taken. In a letter collected in *The Crack-Up*, written to his daughter in the year of his death, 1940, he said: 'I wish now I'd *never* relaxed or looked back – but said at the end of *The Great Gatsby*: "I've found my line – from now on this comes first. This is my immediate duty – without this I am nothing"' (p. 294).

In fact, Fitzgerald had little time to relax after *Gatsby*; his life was demanding and debilitating. It involved his decline from celebrity into obscurity; his alcoholism and bouts of depression; his protracted effort to write another novel; his repeated failure to become an established Hollywood screenwriter; and his need to keep writing short stories to pay for Scottie's upkeep and schooling and for Zelda's psychiatric care after her mental illness became acute in 1930. Once he had felt he was dominating life; now life was dominating him. In 'The Crack-Up', he observes: 'the natural state of the sentient adult is a qualified unhappiness' (p. 84). But he went on trying to be a serious writer. His fourth novel, *Tender is the Night* (1934), tells the story of a brilliant psychiatrist, Dick Diver, who marries a wealthy young woman who has been sexually abused by her father, but finally falls into oblivion. While it did not put him back in the centre of the literary map on its first appearance, its accomplishment can now be appreciated. Fitzgerald's *Crack-Up* essays of 1936, which fellow writers such as Ernest Hemingway (1898–1961) and John Dos Passos (1896–1970) deplored at the time for their self-revelations, now seem not only superbly crafted but also one of the sources of a rich crop of confessional writing by such authors as Robert Lowell (1917–77), Sylvia Plath (1932–63) and William Styron (1925–2006). And *The Love of the Last Tycoon: A Western* – the unfinished novel about Hollywood he was working on when, at the age of 44, he died suddenly of a heart attack in Hollywood on 21 December 1940 – is, even in its incomplete form, a remarkable piece of fiction which shows him developing in new directions and which, had he lived, might have become a masterpiece to equal or surpass *Gatsby*.

As things stand, however, *Gatsby* remains his most popular and most potent novel, constantly attracting new readers and capable of generating an apparently infinite range of meanings. But, while *Gatsby* certainly transcends its time, it is also, like any enduring work of art, very much of its time, emerging in, representing and contributing to a very specific historical context, the decade when, as Fitzgerald put it in 'Early Success' (1937): 'America was going on the greatest, gaudiest spree in history' (*The Crack-Up*, p. 87).

THE HISTORICAL CONTEXT

The multiple, intertwining causes of this great and gaudy spree included the after-effects of the First World War; the impact of prohibition; the growth of organized crime; the emergence of the gangster as an object of fear and fascination; the alarm caused by immigration and the legislative attempt to restrict it; the economic boom; the conspicuous consumption of the rich; the accelerating pace of technological innovation in the areas of transport – the automobile; communications – the telephone; and popular entertainment – the motion picture; the growth of advertising and consumerism; the loosening of sexual and marital constraints; and the emergence of more independent kinds of woman. All these elements feature to a greater or lesser extent in *Gatsby*.

The entry of the USA into the First World War in April 1917 was its first involvement in a major European military conflict and ended decades of isolationism. The American Expeditionary Forces (AEF) were sent to the Western Front and saw action in several significant battles – for example, the Meuse-Argonne offensive: in *Gatsby*, both Nick and Gatsby would have taken part in this. The war took young men abroad, from the New World back to Europe, and some of them – like Nick in *Gatsby* – returned to the USA restless. But if the war caused some social dislocation, it also stimulated the American economy and enhanced the global influence of the USA, confirming it as a world power and diminishing its sense of cultural inferiority to Europe. As Fitzgerald put it in 'Echoes of the Jazz Age' (collected in *The Crack-Up*): 'We were the most powerful nation. Who could tell us any longer what was fashionable and what was fun?' (p. 14).

In the year after the end of hostilities, however, leading Americans tried to tell their fellow citizens that there was one kind of fun they could not have. On January 15 1919, Congress ratified the Eighteenth Amendment, which prohibited the manufacture and sale of alcoholic drinks, and the Volstead Act put it into force. But Prohibition, an outgrowth of old American Puritanism which was designed to create a sober and temperate society, backfired dramatically. It fuelled the rapid growth of organized crime networks engaged in bootlegging – the making and selling of illegal alcoholic drinks – and fostered the emergence of wealthy and powerful gangsters who – like Gatsby – were also active in other criminal fields, such as gambling and bond fraud, and who aspired to social status.

As the example of Arnold Rothstein (1882–1928) in New York, on whom Wolfsheim in *Gatsby* was partly based, or of Al Capone (1899–1947) in Chicago shows, however, gangsterism also provided a means of rapid upward mobility for certain members of some ethnic groups at a time when restrictions on immigration were being tightened. Before the First World War, a larger number of immigrants had come to the USA than ever before, reaching a record high of 1,285,349 in 1907. The National Origins Act of 1924 laid down a quota system based on 2 per cent of the numbers of each nationality in the USA in 1890 which effectively discriminated against those from southern and eastern Europe. The anxiety about ethnic others which issued in such legislation as well as in more overt racist attitudes is evident in *Gatsby* in two of its white Anglo-Saxon male protagonists: Tom and Nick.

Although immigration was being curtailed, the population of the USA was expanding along with the economy in the 1920s. The total of national wealth rose from about $187 million in 1912 to $450 million in 1929. This economic boom was fuelled by new industries, particularly the manufacture of automobiles. In 1895, only four trucks and passenger cars had been made; by 1919, this had risen to 7,565,446 and it went on rising throughout the decade. Automobile production stimulated growth in associated industries, such as road-building, petroleum, iron, steel, rubber and glass. Other industries concerned with communication and entertainment also expanded, selling more telephones, radios and movies. Along with this growth in production went a growth in advertising – the industry in which Fitzgerald found his first job – and in financial services, such as the provision of loans on the instalment plan to enable more people to buy – or to get into debt trying to pay for – the new consumer goods.

The expansion of industry, technological innovation and the greater, though still limited, availability of consumer goods contributed to the important changes in the 1920s in the position and role of women in the USA. Whereas the Eighteenth Amendment which introduced prohibition seemed like a restriction, the Nineteenth Amendment of 1920 was an emancipation, since it gave American women the right to vote for the first time. For those who could afford them, technological innovations and the proliferation of consumer goods lessened the burden of housework, such as washing clothes and cleaning carpets, which had traditionally fallen on women, while the mass production of processed foodstuffs eased the demands of food preparation. The opportunities for female employment increased, although they were still considerably constricted. In advertisements and magazines, a new model for femininity emerged in a social type with which Fitzgerald and his fiction were particularly associated: the flapper. The term had originally been coined in the early twentieth century to refer to a teenage girl with a plait tied in a large bow which flapped against her back as she walked, but in the 1920s it came to refer to a young woman who pursued her own pleasure – including sexual pleasure. A related term, 'baby vamp' – 'vamp' was an abbreviation of 'vampire' – was applied to a young woman who appeared to pursue sexual pleasure in a predatory way, using her sexuality to attract and exploit men. These changes in the position and role of women created a

situation that could be, for both genders, liberating and disturbing at the same time: women would have to negotiate mixed, con-
flicting demands and men would be faced with apparent threats
to their own patriarchal assumptions and privileges. The three
female protagonists of *Gatsby* – Daisy, Jordan and Myrtle – are
all placed in painful, difficult situations as they try to assume a
measure of freedom for themselves, and they present challenges
to the men in their lives, each of whom embodies, in varying
ways, patriarchal ideology: Tom, Gatsby, Nick and George
Wilson.

The economic and cultural changes in 1920s America which
we have considered were complemented by changes in the intellectual and cultural context, and we shall examine these next.

THE INTELLECTUAL AND CULTURAL CONTEXT

The 1920s in America and Europe were a time in which the challenges to traditional ways of understanding the world which had
emerged earlier in the century began to be popularized and more
widely circulated through the mass media of magazines, radio
and the movies. Two of the strongest challenges originated
in Europe: the theory of relativity which Albert Einstein
(1879–1955) had proposed in 1905 was verified by experimental
observations in 1919 and seemed to undermine the concepts of
time and space developed by Isaac Newton (1642–1727), while
the psychoanalytical theories of Sigmund Freud (1856–1939)
suggested that human beings were much less rational than they
had liked to imagine, and that the sexual drive was far more
important than the nineteenth century had been prepared pub-
licly to acknowledge. In the USA itself, William James
(1842–1910), elder brother of the novelist Henry James
(1843–1916) and himself a superb expository writer and lecturer,
had explored the human mind, from a different perspective from
Freud, in *The Principles of Psychology* (1890), where he had
argued that consciousness could not be called a 'chain' or 'train'
but flowed like a river or stream, and that it would therefore be
most appropriately called 'the stream of thought, of consciousness, or of subjective life'. This was the origin of the phrase

'stream of consciousness', used by literary critics to describe a way of writing, most notably exemplified by James Joyce (1882–1941), which aimed to represent the flowing movement of thought. James also developed, in his lectures and the books based on them such as *The Will to Believe* (1897), *Pragmatism* (1907) and *The Meaning of Truth* (1909), the philosophy of pragmatism, which argued that the truth of a proposition depended not on its correspondence to some ultimate reality, but on whether or not it worked in terms of its practical, social or psychological results. On the one hand, this justified holding on to beliefs which could not be decisively proven – religious beliefs, for example – if they seemed to have a beneficial effect upon feelings and behaviour; on the other hand, it appeared to suggest that truth was always relative and provisional. All these ideas suggested that the world and the universe were stranger and more disturbing than had been dreamt of in the nineteenth century.

This sense of strangeness also altered the traditional arts which experienced that great transformation which we now call Modernism. The landmark Modernist works are the painting *Les demoiselles d'Avignon* (*The Maids of Avignon*, 1906–7) by Pablo Picasso (1881–1973); the ballet score *Le sacré du printemps* (*Rite of Spring*, 1913) by Igor Stravinsky (1882–1971); the novel *Ulysses* (1922) by James Joyce; and the poem *The Waste Land* (1922) by T. S. Eliot (1888–1965). All these works fragmented traditional artistic forms in startling ways and helped to create an exciting but challenging cultural context for Fitzgerald's third novel.

THE LITERARY CONTEXT

In terms of literature, the most immediate Modernist influence on *Gatsby* was T. S. Eliot's *The Waste Land*. Eliot's vision of the city and of modern life, his capacity to capture extremes of entropy and ecstasy, his use of the residual traces of myth and religion to provide a shadowy structure for his mobile fragments, all play through *Gatsby*. But Fitzgerald's Modernism was of a quieter kind than Eliot's and the strongest influence on his third novel was the slightly more distant one of Joseph Conrad

(1857–1924). From Conrad, Fitzgerald learned more about how to use a first-person narrator who is a participant-observer and how to scramble chronology effectively. These techniques helped Conrad to pursue the aim he expressed in his preface to *The Nigger of the 'Narcissus'* (1897), which Fitzgerald reread just before he wrote *Gatsby*: 'My task is by the power of the written word to make you hear, to make you feel – it is, before all, to make you *see*.' Fitzgerald also learned more about how to make the reader hear, feel and see from the 'scenic method' employed by Henry James and Edith Wharton (1862–1937); this entailed presenting a series of scenes from which readers could draw their own conclusions rather than having them spelled out by the author. One further important lesson was provided by the symbolic prose of Willa Cather (1873–1947) in *My Ántonia* (1918) and *A Lost Lady* (1923). Fitzgerald's letters show that he knew both these novels and they both have echoes in *Gatsby*. But important though all these influences are, they do not explain Fitzgerald's unique achievement in *Gatsby*; to find out more about that, we must look closely at the text of his novel.

STUDY QUESTIONS FOR CHAPTER 1

1. Although *Gatsby* is not semi-autobiographical in the manner of *This Side of Paradise*, it can be seen as a novel which is indirectly about Fitzgerald's life, in the same way that the film *Citizen Kane* (1940) can be interpreted as a film which is, obliquely, about the life of its director, Orson Welles (1915–85). In what ways might *Gatsby* be about Fitzgerald's life? How useful is a knowledge of Fitzgerald's biography in appreciating the novel?

2. This chapter has suggested a range of elements of 1920s America which figure in *Gatsby*, from the after-effects of the First World War to the emergence of more independent kinds of women. Which of these elements do you think are especially important in Fitzgerald's novel, and why are they important? To what extent does a knowledge of American society in this period help us to understand *Gatsby*?

3. How far do you feel Fitzgerald in *Gatsby* is trying to fulfil the

task of the writer as defined by Joseph Conrad – 'before all, to make you *see*'? Is the 'seeing' of which Conrad speaks of a visual, psychological or moral kind, or a combination of these? Why should a novelist in this period feel that 'making us *see*' is important? (One very interesting way to pursue this question is to read Conrad's *Heart of Darkness* (1902), and to consider how that text 'makes us *see*'. *Heart of Darkness* offers a range of fascinating comparisons and contrasts with *Gatsby* which you could explore further – some of the structural similarities and differences are discussed in the next chapter.

CHAPTER 2

LANGUAGE, STYLE AND FORM

LANGUAGE AND STYLE

The language of *Gatsby* is a rich, complex mixture drawn from a wide variety of sources. These include Romantic poetry; biblical and Christian discourse; the Modernist prose of James Joyce and the Modernist poetry of T. S. Eliot; American slang and educated speech of the 1920s; society guest lists; self-improvement schedules; advertisements; popular song lyrics; and illustrated magazines. All these features are assimilated into a distinctive style which could be called 'Romantic Modernism'. It is a style which combines the images and rhythms derived and developed from nineteenth-century Romantic poetry with the precision, conciseness and topical reference which were becoming the hallmark of Modernist writing in both poetry and prose. In *Gatsby*, Fitzgerald updates Romanticism for the twentieth century and, true to the Modernist demand for high-impact language, packs every sentence with meaning.

In examining the language and style of *Gatsby*, it is important, first of all, to indicate briefly the senses in which the term 'Romantic', with a capital 'R', and 'romantic', with a small 'r', will be employed. 'Romantic' means 'relating to Romanticism' – to those large changes in the tenor of thought and feeling and in artistic practices which began in the late eighteenth century, proved explosively innovative in the early nineteenth century, persisted as a pervasive but increasingly enervated dominant force in high culture until the early twentieth-century, and spread into the new popular culture of newspapers, magazines, movies and songs even as they lost ground in leading-edge high culture. The changes which were involved in Romanticism are complicated and multi-faceted and its leading literary figures included poets as different as Lord Byron (1788–1824), William Blake (1757–1827), Samuel Taylor Coleridge (1772–1834), John Keats (1795–1821), Percy Bysshe Shelley (1792–1822) and William Wordsworth (1770–1850); but broadly speaking, we can say that Romanticism involved an emphasis on imagination rather than intellect, on feeling rather than reason, on subjectivity rather than objectivity, on art rather than science and technology, on transgression rather than conformity, on extremism rather than moderation, on ambiguity rather than clarity, and on seeking transcendence rather than staying within limits. In *Gatsby*, this sense of the 'Romantic' is more important than the everyday modern sense of 'romantic', which means 'related to love, particularly of a sentimental or idealized kind'. *Gatsby* is, however, certainly 'romantic' in this everyday sense as well – indeed it is part of its popular appeal – and the 'Romantic' and the 'romantic' mingle and diverge in all kinds of ways in its pages.

Terms with Romantic and often romantic connotations in *Gatsby* include adjectives such as deathless, enchanted, exhilarating, thrilling and wild, and nouns such as beauty, magic, melancholy, mystery and wonder. In using these terms so extensively in a novel written in the 1920s, Fitzgerald took a tremendous risk: for by this time Romanticism seemed, to the innovative writers of Modernism such as T. S. Eliot, to have long lost its original force and to have become an inert and stultifying remnant of the nineteenth century. The terms of which Fitzgerald was especially fond had become highly suspect in state-of-the-art serious literature. They seemed like devalued creative coinage, worn smooth through overuse and further debased by their exploitation in advertising, magazines and popular fiction. If they were permitted at all, it was only as residual fragments of an irrecoverable past or as objects of ironic deprecation, as in Eliot's *The Waste Land*. At the time of *Gatsby*'s publication, the writing of Ernest Hemingway was almost unknown and had only a few admirers, Fitzgerald among them; but Hemingway's style would emerge as the antithesis of Fitzgerald's and the most radical challenge to it, aiming to strip out Romantic verbiage and get its emotional and aesthetic effects by means of hard, minimalist prose. For Fitzgerald, however, Romantic terms, and the experiences, perceptions and intimations which they evoked, were crucial and he could not simply excise or ring-fence them; instead he aimed to renovate them by assimilating them into a disciplined Modernist style and by letting them share the text with other terms drawn from the contemporary world – from technology and consumer culture, for example.

For instance, Fitzgerald challenges the conventional Romantic opposition between technology and art, the machine and the imagination, by drawing on technological imagery to help evoke Romantic perspectives and perceptions – which are, however, themselves inevitably modified in the process. At the start of *Gatsby*, for example, Nick likens Gatsby's enhanced responsiveness to the possibilities of life to a machine which registers distant earthquakes (p. 8) – a seismograph. A little later, he takes one of the commonplaces of Romantic and lyric poetry – the growth of leaves on the summer trees – and compares them to the way things grow 'in fast movies' – films which show the growth of a flower or tree compressed into a few minutes (p. 9). Technology here is not opposed to nature but provides an image through which its processes can be quickly grasped and conveyed. Later in the novel (though earlier in its fictional time), we learn that Daisy's house in Louisville hints to Second Lieutenant Gatsby of 'romances' that are 'fresh and breathing and redolent of this year's shining motor-cars' (p. 141); the imagery here draws not only on the technology of the automobile but also on consumer culture, on advertising. This is also the case when Nick, meeting Jordan to say goodbye to her for the last time and still 'half in love with her' (p. 169), thinks that she looks like 'a good illustration' in a magazine (p. 168) – a simile that echoes the moment during his first meeting with her when he recalls that he has seen her many times in the 'rotogravure' (p. 23) – a magazine or newspaper with photographs printed by means of what was, in early-twentieth-century terms, a high-tech system that employed a rotary press with intaglio (engraved) cylinders. It might be said that the use of such imagery, particularly in the cases of Jordan and Daisy, does not so much renovate Romanticism – or the 'romantic' – as show that it has become reduced to mechanical superficiality in the modern age; but while the way in which Fitzgerald deploys these images certainly raises the question of whether a valid Romanticism is still possible in the contemporary world, it does not imply that the question can only be answered in the negative. Fitzgerald's combination, in his style, of Romantic imagery and attitudes with imagery drawn from modern technology and consumer culture puts two opposed ideas into play: the idea that Romanticism is irretrievable for modernity, and the idea that modernity provides new Romantic possibilities.

Compared to its copious use of Romantic vocabulary, *Gatsby* employs Christian terms sparingly, but it does so at strategic points in the narrative which give those terms especially strong significance. Above all, they are crucial to Nick's account of Gatsby's relationship with Daisy and suggest its quasi-religious nature. Just before Gatsby kisses her for the first time, he sees, out of the corner of his eye, that the blocks of the sidewalk form a ladder which climbs to 'a secret place above the trees' (p. 106); the ladder alludes to Jacob's dream, in the Old Testament book of Genesis, of a ladder rising from earth up to heaven, with the angels of God ascending and descending on it (Gen. 28.12). It is this ladder and its promise which Gatsby knows he will renounce when he kisses Daisy: 'his mind would never romp again like the mind of God' (p. 107) – we can see, in the application of the verb 'romp' applied to the mind of God, one of Fitzgerald's unusual juxtapositions. But the kiss will itself be a kind of religious experience, an embodiment like that of Christ when he descended to earth: 'At his lips' touch she blossomed for him like a flower and the *incarnation* was complete' (p. 107, my italics). The kiss eventually leads to the full physical consummation of his relationship with Daisy and he finds, probably to his own surprise, that this consummation has committed him to pursuing a 'grail' (p. 142): in medieval legend, the grail was the cup or platter which Christ used at the Last Supper and which Joseph of Arimathea employed as a receptacle for Christ's blood.

The most extended and significant use of Christian language in *Gatsby* occurs, however, when Nick is describing, in Chapter 6, the young Gatsby's rejection of his parents and his change of name; this passage also invokes classical philosophy and includes romantic vocabulary.

The truth was that Jay Gatsby of West Egg, Long Island, sprang from his Platonic conception of himself. He was a son of God – a phrase which, if it means anything, means just that – and he must be about His Father's business, the service of a vast, vulgar and meretricious beauty.' (p. 95).

The first sentence refers to the ancient Greek philosopher Plato (*c*.429–347 BC) and his idea that there was a world of ideal forms of which the material world was an imperfect representation: the implication is that Gatsby created an ideal form of himself which he then tried to represent in the material world – an attempt which was, given the nature of the material world, bound to fail. But this reference to Plato and Gatsby could also be seen to encompass a reference to the American Dream: for it could be said that the USA sprang from its Platonic conception of itself: that it attempted to put into practice the ideals inscribed in the American Declaration of Independence – and, perhaps inevitably, failed.

The second sentence introduces explicit references to Christianity: Christ is the son of God, and in the New Testament Gospel of St Luke (2.42–52) it is the 12-year-old Christ who, without telling his parents, goes to hear and question the doctors in the temple in Jerusalem and who, when his parents find him and Mary asks why he has caused his parents sorrow by disappearing in such a way, replies: 'wist [know] ye not that I must be about my Father's business?'. These allusions to Plato and Christ place Gatsby in a very exalted frame of reference; but the final phrase of the second sentence perturbs the picture by defining the nature of the business in which he must engage in ambiguous terms, as 'the service of a vast, vulgar and meretricious beauty'. Here a romantic noun which denotes aesthetic and erotic experience, 'beauty', and a romantic adjective which indicates huge size, 'vast', are linked with 'vulgar' – a term whose older meaning is 'of the people' but which has come to denote a lack of taste – and 'meretricious', which means 'showily but falsely attractive' (and its archaic meaning, 'characteristic of a prostitute', also has relevance here).

The only character in *Gatsby* who calls on God directly is George Wilson, in his agonized vigil after Myrtle's death. But Wilson's God is both strange and estranged. In his initial extremity of distress he seems to fragment God when he repeatedly splits His name into two – 'Ga-od' (p. 132) – and unwittingly makes the first syllable of the broken name of the divinity sound like the start of a name he does not yet seem to know but will soon learn, with lethal consequences: '*Ga*-tsby'. In the early hours of the morning, in response to Michaelis's reiterated question as to whether he is a member of a Christian church, he replies that he does not belong to any. In a final, uncanny moment, as the oculist's billboard becomes visible in the blue dawn, he seems to conflate God with the eyes of Dr Eckleburg (p. 152).

While Christian language and imagery is reserved for especially significant moments in *Gatsby*, there is another strand of vocabulary in the novel which is also important but occurs more often: colour adjectives. Listed in the order of the frequency of their occurrence, these include white (47 times), yellow (22), blue (22), green (17), red (9) and pink (6). They help to give *Gatsby* its vivid and varied visual allure and also contribute significantly to its symbolism. There is, however, no simple correlation between the symbolic and thematic importance of a colour term in the novel as a whole and the number of times it appears, and no simple correspondence between a specific colour term and a particular meaning; rather, the colours alter in their significance according to their contexts, linked sometimes with the positive, sometimes with the negative, and sometimes with the ambivalent.

Consider, for example, green, which is perhaps the most important colour term in *Gatsby*, though not the most frequent one. It is the colour of aspiration and desire and covers both Daisy and America, nature and culture, the 'fresh, green breast of the new world' (p. 171) and its technological equivalent, the green light at the end of Daisy's dock. Jordan Baker's voice usually comes across on the phone to Nick as if it were a divot – a piece of turf which a golf club cuts out in making a stroke – from a green golf course (p. 147); the fresh green breast of the new world has become a carefully cultivated sward on which the leisure class may disport itself. But traditionally green is also the colour of envy and jealousy, and these associations play into its significance in *Gatsby* as well. The fresh green breast of the new world was an open invitation to human rapacity; the green light lures Gatsby to his death because it represents a woman whose voice is full of money; according to Nick, Jordan Baker lies and cheats at golf because she always has to have the upper hand. Other points in the novel at which green occurs reinforce its negative connotations. Green is the colour of the upholstery of Gatsby's car – the vehicle which the newspaper will later call the 'death-car' and which Michaelis describes as light green to the first policeman he sees after the accident (p. 131). When Tom and Nick stop at Wilson's garage on the way into New York and the confrontation at the Plaza Hotel, Wilson's face, when he comes out into the sunlight, is green (p. 117).

In *Gatsby*'s use of colour terms, aspects of the real world as we perceive it – colours – take on, within the fictional world of the novel, extra meanings over and above their primary meaning; these extra meanings, however, cannot be fully articulated or finally fixed and limited and they may sometimes appear inconsistent and contradictory. In these respects, they exemplify the way in which symbolism works in *Gatsby*: as well as colours, there are a host of other features of the real world which, as they are evoked in the novel, assume extra meanings and thus function as symbols. These symbols are drawn from the human body, from the supernatural, from nature and from technology, and include eyes, noses, breasts, breath, ghosts, automobiles, trains, ships, telephones, ashes, heat, water, flowers, the sun, the moon and eggs. To increase our understanding of how these work, we shall look at the most memorable of them: eyes.

The importance of this symbol in *Gatsby* is epitomized by the eyes of Doctor T. J. Eckleburg. This symbol straddles the contemporary commercial world and the world of traditional religious faith, in a way that both brings them together and high-lights the disjunction between them: the eyes are on a billboard, advertising an optician's practice in Queens which is long since defunct; but they become, in Wilson's eyes, the eyes of God, who sees all. On one level, this is ironic: in the early twentieth century, God has absconded, is dead, has become no more than an adver-tisement image, an illusory representation on a flat surface with nothing but the valley of ashes behind it; but the moment in which Wilson identifies the image as God is sufficiently chilling to allow the reader momentarily to share his perception and to raise the possibility that an observing, judging presence may still be there, but not necessarily a compassionate or merciful one. The billboard eyes can be linked with other eyes in the novel – particularly Owl Eyes, the man with huge owl-eyed spectacles who assesses Gatsby's achievement as an illusionist when he inspects the books in his library (pp. 46–7), who reappears a little later as a passenger in the coupé driven by a drunken guest which has gone into the ditch and had its wheel torn off (pp. 54–5), who is the only party guest apart from Nick to come to Gatsby's funeral and who pronounces a curt epitaph on the dead man: 'The poor son-of-a-bitch' (pp. 165–6).

Then there are Daisy's eyes, which for Gatsby are the eyes of judgement: when he shows her round his mansion for the first time, he looks at her constantly and Nick, looking at him, infers that he revalues 'everything in his house according to the measure of response it drew from her well-loved eyes' (p. 88); her eyes also make Nick look at Gatsby's guests and the whole social world of West Egg differently, an experience which lowers his spirits. 'It is invariably saddening to look through new eyes at things upon which you have expended your own powers of adjustment' (pp. 100–1). Nick's own eyes are those of the observer-participant, and perhaps to some extent can be seen as Fitzgerald's version of Tiresias, the ancient bisexual sage who sees and foresuffers all in Eliot's *The Waste Land*. His eyes are perhaps also those of the voyeur: on his first visit to the Buchanan mansion, when the phone rings again as Tom, Daisy, Jordan and Nick are at dinner, Nick is aware that he wants 'to look squarely at everyone, and yet to avoid all eyes' (pp. 20–1);

and in New York, he exemplifies 'the restless eye', satisfied, like a movie watcher, by 'the constant flicker of men and women and machines' (p. 57). Near the end of the novel, he declares: 'After Gatsby's death, the East was haunted for me ... distorted beyond my eyes' power of correction' (p. 167) – a remark which, taken with other elements of *Gatsby*, raises doubts about Nick's reliability as a narrator, the accuracy of his eyes.

We can see, then, that the symbolism of eyes has many meanings in *Gatsby*; but it also, like the other key symbols, contributes to the structure of the novel. For the power of *Gatsby* is not due only to its language and style, remarkable though they are; it is also due to its form, and we shall now examine this more closely.

FORM

As well as supplying a rich range of extra meanings, the symbols in *Gatsby* contribute to the form of Fitzgerald's novel by helping to bind it together through their recurrence at strategic points: the faceless eyes of Eckleburg rise up, blue and gigantic, at the start of Chapter 2; recur, briefly but ominously, in Chapter 8 during Tom and Nick's journey into New York; and return with enormous force when they emerge as the eyes of God in the blue quickening of the dawn after Myrtle's death. The primary binding agent of *Gatsby*, however, is its narrator, Nick Carraway. As we observed in the last chapter, Fitzgerald had learned much from Joseph Conrad about the possibilities of a first-person narrator who is both observer and participant and who is involved in a close and complex way with a man who cannot tell his own story because he is dead. Despite the differences in terms of characters and settings between *Gatsby* and Conrad's *Heart of Darkness*, the two narratives are, in a structural sense, similar: the positions of both Nick and Marlow in relation to their own stories could be summed up by Nick's comment on his dual, divided role in the scene at Myrtle's apartment when he imagines how its lighted windows would look to a casual observer in the streets below: 'I was within and without' (p. 37). But Nick is 'without', not only because of the inner reserve which operates even when he is in the thick of a situation, but also, like Marlow, because of the distance in time which separates him from the events he describes; unlike Marlow, however, he is, supposedly, recreating those events through the act of writing and this lends another dimension to his detachment. Whereas *Heart of Darkness* starts and ends with another, anonymous narrator, one of Marlow's listeners, who provides a frame for the story that Marlow tells, Nick provides his own frame, presenting himself as the voice of experience and setting himself at a geographical, cultural and temporal distance from the East from which he returned the previous autumn in a rigid and withdrawn state of mind. In contrast to Marlow in *Heart of Darkness*, Nick has no listeners around him and he never indicates the nature of his potential audience – perhaps it is himself, since his revelations would have an explosive impact if they were true and he published them – and he does not explicitly indicate in this opening section that he intends to tell, or write, a story. But in Chapter 3, after the section break which ends his portrayal of Gatsby's party, he clearly announces himself as the supposed writer – and reader – of the narrative, when he remarks that, reading over what he has written, he sees how his account has falsified the reality of his life at the time by focusing only on those events which relate to the story of Gatsby and which, it is implied, have only assumed in retrospect the narrative significance they now enjoy.

Nick makes only two further explicit references to himself as narrator, in Chapters 6 and 8, and on both those occasions he draws attention to his alteration of the chronological order of events. In doing this, he highlights another key aspect of the narrative form of *Gatsby*: its manipulation of time. In examining this aspect of the novel, it is illuminating first of all to reconstruct the story of Gatsby's earlier life in chronological order from his birth up to the time that Nick first sees him, making use of and rearranging the flashbacks and other relevant references to the past in the novel. Around 1890, James Gatz is born to poor parents in the Midwest, in North Dakota; as an adolescent, he finds that his ambitions are developing and he inwardly rejects his parents and engages in extravagant fantasies about his future. He goes to St Olaf's, a small Lutheran College in southern Minnesota, intending to study and support himself by working as a janitor; but this humble approach does not correspond to his own sense of his potential, and he leaves after two weeks. He then becomes a kind of beachcomber and odd-job man, working as a clam-digger, salmon-fisher or anything else that enables him to find food and accommodation. In about 1907, when he is 17, he sees Dan Cody's yacht anchor over a dangerous flat on Lake Superior and rows out to warn him about it; when Cody asks him his name he gives it, for the first time, as Jay Gatsby. Cody takes him on as a kind of personal assistant and jack-of-all-trades and Gatsby works for him for five years, until around 1912. In that year, one night in Boston, a lady called Ella Kaye comes aboard the yacht, and Cody dies a week later, although no information is given about the cause of his death. He leaves Gatsby 25 thousand dollars, but Gatsby never gets it; the will is declared invalid and the remains of Cody's millions go to Ella Kaye.

We have no information about Gatsby's life from 1912 until the time he enters the army. It is while he is a second lieutenant stationed in Camp Taylor in Louisville that he starts going to Daisy's house with other officers, and then begins to visit on his own. One October night, he makes love to Daisy, and finds that he feels married to her and has committed himself to the pursuit of a 'grail'. Their love affair continues until he is sent off to the war in Europe. He has been promoted to captain by the time he is sent to the front and after the Argonne battles he is promoted to major, placed in command of his division's machine guns and decorated with medals. When the armistice is declared, he tries to get home but ends up going to Oxford for five months instead. While he is at Oxford, he receives a letter telling him that Daisy is to marry Tom Buchanan. While Daisy and Tom are on their honeymoon, he returns to Louisville for a nostalgic and melancholy week and then goes to New York. Still wearing his army uniform because he has no money to buy civilian clothes, he walks into Winebrenner's poolroom in New York asking for a job; he has had nothing to eat for two days. Wolfshiem sees him there, buys him a meal, and puts him to work, presumably using him as a front for various criminal activities. No further hard facts about those activities are given and we are told no more about how Gatsby gets to the position he is in when Nick first meets him.

To tell the story of Gatsby's earlier life in this way is to highlight how very different it seems in the novel, when it emerges through flashbacks. In a sense, of course, almost all of *Gatsby* is a prolonged flashback: according to the opening section of the novel, Nick is recalling events that happened the previous year (p. 8), and although by the last chapter of the novel the time-lapse seems to have extended to two years (p. 155), this apparent inconsistency could be explained by saying that it has taken Nick a year to write his story. Within this prolonged flashback, other, shorter flashbacks are inserted. In Chapter 4, there is Jordan Baker's story, told in the first person, of the young Daisy Fay, her encounter with the young Gatsby, her marriage to Tom, his early infidelity with a chambermaid at the Santa Barbara Hotel, and the birth of Tom and Daisy's daughter, Pammie (pp. 72–5). In Chapter 6, Nick provides, near the start of the chapter, a summary of Gatsby's years with Dan Cody (pp. 94–7), and then concludes the chapter with an account of the first time Gatsby kissed Daisy (pp. 106–7). In Chapter 8, Nick interrupts his account of the morning of Gatsby's death with a flashback based on what Gatsby supposedly told him that morning. This flashback covers the development and consummation of Gatsby's relationship with Daisy in Louisville, his success in the war, his going to Oxford, Daisy's marriage to Tom, and Gatsby's brief return to Louisville (pp. 141–6). The final fragment of Gatsby's story is supplied in Chapter 9, when Wolfshiem tells Nick he first met Gatsby in Winebrenner's poolroom. Few details of what working with Wolfshiem involved are given, however; as we have already mentioned, there is still a large gap in Gatsby's story between the point at which Wolfshiem takes him up and his emergence as the lavish party-giver of West Egg; the source of Gatsby's wealth remains a mystery, though there are hints that he is engaged in a range of lucrative criminal activities – bootlegging, fixing the results of sporting events in order to win bets on them, and dealing in stolen bonds. But the reader who seeks traditional narrative satisfactions and wants to know the whole truth about the novel's protagonist will be thwarted: *Gatsby* will not fill in all the gaps.

Apart from the smaller timeshift to the scene between Michaelis and Wilson, *Gatsby* does provide one more flashback, however, and it is a surprising one. As we approach the closing pages – the point at which, in a more traditional narrative, we might have expected to receive some definitive truth, or at least some more information, about Gatsby – the focus shifts to Nick and a significant part of his past. This flashback does not relate a one-off episode but rolls features of a repeated experience into a single vivid recollection – lovingly and sharply evoked, laden with nostalgia – of Nick's Christmas returns by train, as a schoolboy and then a college student, to the Middle West. It is a return he has now made again, perhaps for good, and the flashback concludes with an attempt to assimilate the characters whose conflicts have had lethal consequences – Tom, Gatsby, Daisy, Jordan and Nick himself – into an imaginary unity on the basis of their common Midwest origin: 'I see now that this has been a story of the West, after all – Tom and Gatsby, Daisy and Jordan and I, were all Westerners' (p. 167). It is as if, by the power of Nick's narrative, their forward movement has led them finally back to their beginnings.

This ring of return anticipates the huge and breathtaking flashback that will conclude the novel, a flashback not to an episode in an individual's past but to the prehistory of the USA itself and to the idea that the attempt to reach the future is countered by a force that drives us endlessly back to the past. This conclusion implies that the shuffling of chronology in *Gatsby* is not only a technical device to sharpen the interest of the reader and to create contrasts and similarities between earlier and later events in the life of its eponymous protagonist: the shifting between past and present is a part of the novel's concern with truth and appearance and its questioning of the dominant Western notion that earthly reality lies in linear time, in forward movement, in the attainment of future goals.

As well as the use of participant-observer narrator and the rearrangement of linear time, *Gatsby* also employs the scenic method we discussed in the previous chapter – the method, developed by Henry James and taken up by Edith Wharton and Willa Cather, which favours 'showing' the reader, by a series of dramatized scenes, rather than telling them by means of an omniscient narrator. In fact the narrator of *Gatsby*, while not omniscient, does 'tell' us quite a lot, but the novel combines his commentary with vivid scenes that demonstrate Fitzgerald's ability to speed up or slow down time, to build up a sense of tension and conflict, and to capture different ways of speaking. These scenes are made more realistic, and dramatic, by their focus on the difficulty the characters have in connecting with one another or even with themselves; a difficulty ironically counter-pointed by the presence, in several of them, of the most up-to-date technological means of human connection available at the time: the telephone. It is the 'shrill metallic urgency' (p. 21) of this extra guest, which enables Myrtle's voice to invade the Buchanan mansion, that causes Nick's first visit to Daisy, Tom and Jordan to collapse into 'broken fragments (p. 20) – and 'broken fragments' could be a good description of all the extended scenes in *Gatsby*, in which characters talk at cross-purposes, fail to listen or reply to one another, find it difficult or impossible to finish what they are saying, and only truly connect through conflict – when Tom breaks Myrtle's nose, when Tom and Gatsby face off in the Plaza Hotel. In the dialogue of these scenes, Fitzgerald employs, at strategic moments, the rhetorical device of aposiopesis, in which a speech is suddenly broken off and the sentence left unfin-ished; the breaking-off is usually marked by a dash, one of Fitzgerald's favourite punctuation marks, which is also used a great deal in Nick's prose narrative in preference to semicolons or colons and which helps to give a sense of immediacy and nervous energy to Nick's discourse. On one level, the use of aposiopesis in the dialogue of *Gatsby* serves, as it often does in fiction, to rein-force an impression of verisimilitude, echoing the way in which sentences are often left unfinished in real-life conversations. On another level, more integrally related to the themes of the book, it indicates the difficulty the characters have in articulating them-selves and communicating with one another.

There are four especially striking aposiopeses in the novel: Myrtle's 'Daisy! Dai—' which breaks off when Tom breaks her nose (p. 39); Gatsby's laughing 'I can't– when I try to—' which breaks off when Gatsby cannot find the words to express his emotions on meeting Daisy again for the first time after almost five years (p. 89); Daisy's words to Gatsby in the Plaza Hotel scene just after she has made it obliquely but unmistakably clear to Tom that she loves Gatsby: 'You resemble the advertisement of the man . . . You know the advertisement of the man—' (p. 114) which breaks off when she cannot find an image which is equal to what she feels for Gatsby; and Gatsby's desperate attempt, in the same scene, to evade the reality of Daisy's refusal to say that she never loved Tom: 'I want to speak to Daisy alone . . . She's all excited now—' (p. 126) which breaks off when Daisy admits that she cannot comply with Gatsby's demand. The end of the Plaza Hotel scene once more collapses into 'broken fragments'; and this time the damage is irreparable.

Nick's phrase 'broken fragments' echoes Eliot's line near the end of *The Waste Land*: 'These fragments I have shored against my ruins' (l. 430). In *Gatsby*, Fitzgerald, as a novelist, faced the challenge that Eliot, as a poet, faced in *The Waste Land*: how to find an artistic form which would adequately represent the fragmentation of modern life without itself falling to bits. Fitzgerald's response was to develop, both at the levels of language and style, and at the level of form, the techniques of Conrad, James, Wharton, Cather and Eliot himself and to forge, in *Gatsby*, a unique work which transcended these influences and succeeded in representing fragmentation in a way that was aesthetically satisfying but which did not evade engagement with large themes. We shall explore these themes in the next chapter.

STUDY QUESTIONS FOR CHAPTER 2

1. In its discussion of colour terms in *Gatsby*, this chapter has focused on green, but it also mentions other recurrent colours in the novel, especially white, yellow and blue. Find some significant examples of colours, other than green, which recur in *Gatsby* and consider what they contribute to the specific passages in which they feature and to the overall symbolic and thematic structure of the novel.

2. What are the advantages and disadvantages of using a first-person narrator in *Gatsby*? What would the story gain and/or lose if it were told by more than one first-person narrator – for example, Nick and Daisy – or in the third person by an omniscient narrator? (A stimulating way to pursue this question is to try to rewrite scenes from the novel from the viewpoints of other characters or an omniscient narrator – for example, the scene near the end of Chapter 7 in which Nick sees Tom and Daisy through the pantry window.)

3. Explore further what the 'scenic method' contributes to the novel by focusing on specific scenes – for instance, the gathering in Myrtle's apartment in Chapter 2 or the confrontation in the Plaza Hotel in Chapter 7 – and examining how these scenes employ dialogue and description to reveal character, develop the action of the story, and contribute to its themes.

CHAPTER 3

READING THE TEXT

As our examination of the language, style and form of *Gatsby* in the previous chapter has suggested, the novel is a tightly written, carefully structured work in which every sentence is packed with meaning. Its richness has given rise to many interpretations, and we shall survey the critical response to the novel in the next chapter; in this chapter, we shall focus on six key themes which seem especially important in exploring *Gatsby* from the vantage point of the twenty-first century. These themes are:

1. Romanticism
2. America: Dream and History
3. America: The 1920s
4. Money
5. Sexuality and Gender
6. Appearance and Reality

These themes are interwoven in *Gatsby* and cannot easily be separated. For the purposes of analysis, however, we shall take each of them in turn. The start of each section will identify criticism related to its theme which is discussed in the next chapter. There will then be an exploration of each theme which will incorporate a close reading of a particularly relevant passage from the novel. The last section of this chapter will include discussion points, questions and suggestions for further study.

ROMANTICISM

(See discussion of Mizener and Troy in Chapter 4, and 'Romanticism' section of Chapter 6.)

The previous chapter of this guide gave a broad definition of Romanticism as a cultural and artistic movement which valued imagination over intellect, feeling over reason, subjectivity over objectivity, art over science and technology, transgression over conformity, extremism over moderation, ambiguity over clarity, and the quest for transcendence over the respect for limits. It emerged in the later eighteenth century and dominated the nineteenth century but, by the early twentieth century, it seemed bankrupt. Fitzgerald, however, in *Gatsby*, forged a style which could use Romantic vocabulary without seeming regressive; he did so by incorporating it into disciplined prose which had the precision and concentration characteristic of the best Modernist writing, and by bringing it into conjunction with vocabulary and imagery drawn from modern life. But Romanticism in *Gatsby* is not just a matter of style: it is a central theme of the novel. *Gatsby* investigates two key aspects of Romanticism. One aspect is historical: the fate of Romanticism in a specific time and place, America in the 1920s; the other is universal: its dependence on disappointment.

The issue of the fate of Romanticism in modern America is focused in *Gatsby* by two allusions to Keats. In Chapter 1, during Nick's first visit to the Buchanan mansion, Daisy twice uses the adjective 'romantic' to describe the view when she looks outdoors and sees a bird which she suggests must be a nightingale that has travelled over on the Cunard or White Star shipping line (p. 20). In this situation, the meaning of the term 'romantic' hovers between the two senses that we identified in the previous chapter; on one level, it relates to love – or, more precisely, it is an oblique and ironic reference to Tom's affair with Myrtle, to whom he has just been speaking on the phone; on another level, it relates to Romanticism, since the mention of a nightingale calls up Keats's 'Ode to a Nightingale' (1820), a poem which poignantly evokes the transience of beauty and the desire for death. The allusion to Keats's 'Ode' may seem to invite an ironic comparison between an intense founding vision and a vapid stock response; but there is more to it than that.

Daisy's remark that the nightingale must have travelled over by ship is not simply a piece of whimsy; nightingales are not native to America and if there really had been one in her garden, it would have had to have come from elsewhere. Looked at in this way, the allusion can be seen as a reference to the difficulty of translating Romanticism from England to the USA. That difficulty is heightened by Daisy's reference to the shipping lines, which were capitalist companies run for profit; the implication is that Romanticism, if it comes to the USA, cannot evade commercial considerations.

Gatsby does not propose, however, that Romanticism must necessarily be wholly debased in its translation to modern America. The creative possibilities of positive translation are illustrated by a second allusion to Keats which Fitzgerald himself highlighted in a letter to his daughter when he challenged her to find, in stanza four of Keats's 'Ode to a Nightingale' – the stanza which gave him the title for *Tender is the Night* – some lines which he adapted for *Gatsby*. These are the concluding lines of the stanza: 'But here there is no light, / Save what from heaven is with the breezes blown / Through verdurous glooms and winding mossy ways.' Near the end of Chapter 5 of the novel, when Gatsby and Daisy have been reunited for the first time and they are in the music room of his mansion, these lines become: 'He lit Daisy's cigarette from a trembling match, and sat down with her on a couch far across the room, where there was no light save what the gleaming floor bounced in from the hall' (pp. 91–2). The differences between the language used and the situation evoked in Keats's 'Ode' and in Fitzgerald's novel are indicative of more general differences between early-nineteenth-century English Romanticism and early-twentieth-century American Romanticism. Whereas the Keats poem is set out of doors, the Gatsby scene is indoors; Keats's light comes from 'heaven' – from the skies, but also, it is implied, from some supernatural and quasi-divine region – and is carried on the breeze, whereas Gatsby's light comes from electricity – a few moments before, he has flipped a switch at the top of the stairs – and it is reflected from below – presumably from the hall floor – rather than brought from above through natural means. The verb 'blown' in the Keats stanza is replaced by 'bounced', an unusual verb in this context, which gives the light the resilience of a hard-struck tennis ball. Fitzgerald's adaptation of the Keats lines provides a compressed example of the way in which *Gatsby* creatively reconstructs Romanticism in a different cultural space.

This creative reconstruction takes place throughout the novel and effectively demonstrates the continuing potential of Romanticism. This is not to diminish the fact that *Gatsby* shows, unsparingly, that Romanticism, in early-twentieth-century America, is bound up with capitalism, with materialism, with brutality, with waste, with selfishness, with sexual infidelity and predatoriness; but it still affirms the value of Romantic aspiration. But that aspiration also presents another kind of problem, one that is not specific to twentieth-century America: for there is a sense that such aspiration is doomed to disappointment: that it can never attain its goal because the desirability of that goal depends on its separation from the desiring subject. Romantic desire is insatiable; once satiated, it ceases to be Romantic desire. A passage which epitomizes this contradiction occurs in Chapter 5 when, at the end of the afternoon on which Gatsby and Daisy are reunited after almost five years, Nick speculates on what Gatsby may be feeling:

> As I went over to say goodbye I saw that the expression of bewilderment had come back into Gatsby's face, as though a faint doubt had occurred to him as to the quality of his present happiness. Almost five years! There must have been moments even that afternoon when Daisy tumbled short of his dreams – not through her own fault, but because of the colossal vitality of his illusion. It had gone beyond her, beyond everything. He had thrown himself into it with a creative passion, adding to it all the time, decking it out with every bright feather that drifted his way. No amount of fire or freshness can challenge what a man can store up in his ghostly heart. (pp. 92–3)

This passage provides a good example of the way in which Nick, although a first-person narrator rather than an omniscient one, can suggest the inner workings of the minds of other characters, especially Gatsby's, by entering imaginatively into them. Nick infers from an outward sign which he observes – Gatsby's expression of bewilderment – that Gatsby faintly doubts the quality of the happiness he feels. The word 'doubt' sounds an ominous note, especially if we link it with the idea cited in the previous chapter – that for Gatsby, Daisy was a 'grail' (p. 142), a quasi-sacred object of devotion. In the context of Gatsby's semi-religious devotion to Daisy, 'doubt' implies that Gatsby is starting to lose his faith. 'Quality' is also a significant term: it means the standard of one thing measured against other similar things and it suggests here that Gatsby is starting to evaluate his happiness and finding that it does not quite measure up to the happiness which he had imagined his reunion with Daisy would bring.

The exclamation 'Almost five years!' seems to plunge the reader, momentarily, into Gatsby's mind. It is, in fact, uncertain whether we should attribute the phrase to Nick or Gatsby; but because it is in direct speech, it gives a sense of immediacy, as if Nick were no longer indirectly relating his own or Gatsby's thoughts but giving them as they occurred. The next sentence draws back from such immediacy, but by using the verb 'must have', it gives a sense of authority to what follows, making it seem that it is very likely that Gatsby felt this. 'Must have' is a form of phrasing that occurs at other significant moments in the novel, most notably in Nick's speculation, near the end of Chapter 8, about how Gatsby 'must have felt' on the last day of his life, after the final collapse of his Romantic, and romantic, dream (pp. 153–4). Nick's belief that he knows what 'must have' been going on inside Gatsby's head demonstrates the strength of his identification with Gatsby – or, more precisely, with his idea of Gatsby.

In specifying what Gatsby's feelings 'must have' been, Nick's substitution of the verb 'tumbled short' for the more usual 'fell short' is characteristic of the surprising use of language in the novel; and the change of verb, suggesting a more sudden and dramatic descent than a mere fall, emphasizes Gatsby's disappointment. Nick makes it clear, however, that Daisy is not to be blamed for this disappointment; the fault lies with the 'colossal vitality' of Gatsby's illusion. Once again, this is a surprising combination of words. 'Colossal' suggests something huge, much larger than life, with the monumental grandeur of an ancient Egyptian statue but perhaps also with the inflated and vain ambition symbolized by the broken colossus in Shelley's poem 'Ozymandias'. 'Vitality' connotes energy and activity in the present – the only other times it is used in *Gatsby* are in relation to Myrtle Wilson. 'Illusion', however, suggests a false idea or belief and the next sentence implies that it has got hopelessly out of proportion. But if this seems to lead towards a final, dismissive judgement that Gatsby is deluded, the term 'creative passion' in the following sentence turns in another direction, implying that Gatsby is possessed, not so much of an illusion, but of an artistic, even religious impulse – one meaning of 'passion' is the suffering and death of Christ, and this links up with the other Christian imagery related to Gatsby in the novel. These exalted implications are reduced by the next sentence, which suggests that Gatsby lacks discrimination and is attracted by the fragile, insubstantial allure of 'bright feathers'; the religious associations are revived, however, by the adjective 'ghostly', which links up with the other references to 'ghosts' in the novel but also retains traces of the older meaning of 'ghost': spirit or soul. But here the 'ghostly heart' may not so much be spirit or soul as the Romantic imagination, which is stronger than the sensuous ('fire') or the new ('freshness').

This passage is a microcosm of the complex way in which *Gatsby* treats the theme of Romanticism. Within the space of a fairly short paragraph, a range of attitudes have been referenced. Romanticism is huge, energetic, delusive, excessive, creative, Christlike, ornamented, and stronger than the pleasures of the senses and the lure of novelty. And it is this complex, multifaceted contradictory Romanticism that is embodied in Gatsby himself and pervades the novel of which he is the protagonist. It is a Romanticism which enters into and overlaps with a second key theme of *Gatsby*: the American Dream and American history.

AMERICA: DREAM AND HISTORY

(See discussion of Bewley, Bicknell, Callahan, Fussell and Trilling in Chapter 4, and 'America: Dream and History' section of Chapter 6.)

Gatsby does not use the term 'American Dream', and the major warrant for interpreting it as a novel on this theme is the famous passage which, in the original manuscript, was situated at the end of the first chapter but which now concludes the novel as a whole. On his last night at West Egg, Nick is lying on the beach at night after visiting Gatsby's forsaken mansion:

> Most of the big shore places were closed now and there were hardly any lights except the shadowy, moving glow of a ferry-boat across the Sound. And as the moon rose higher the inessential houses began to melt away until gradually I became aware of the old island here that flowered once for Dutch sailors' eyes – a fresh, green breast of the new world. Its vanished trees, the trees that had made way for Gatsby's house, had once pandered in whispers to the last and greatest of all human dreams; for a transitory enchanted moment man must have held his breath in the presence of this continent, compelled into an aesthetic contemplation he neither understood nor desired, face to face for the last time in history with something commensurate to his capacity for wonder.
>
> And as I sat there brooding on the old, unknown world, I thought of Gatsby's wonder when he first picked out the green light at the end of Daisy's dock. He had come a long way to this blue lawn, and his dream must have seemed so close that he could hardly fail to grasp it. He did not know that it was already behind him, somewhere back in that vast obscurity beyond the city, where the dark fields of the republic rolled on under the night. (p. 171)

In this passage, we see the culminating evidence of Nick's romanticism – but it is a romanticism specifically linked to the pre-history of the USA. At night, on the margin between the primal elements of earth and water, a transformation takes place that is explicable in realistic terms but also has a magical quality, as the too, too solid houses 'melt' and give way to a vision of a past time, a founding moment. In the second sentence of the passage, three important symbols in *Gatsby* – eyes, flowers and breasts – and one important colour term – green – come together: it is the *eyes* of the sailors for which the island *flowers* and then becomes, in a rapid metamorphosis in which the later form retains the after-image of the earlier, 'a fresh, *green breast* of the new world' – a metaphor which combines the maternal, erotic, natural and territorial. The use of the word 'breast' here contrasts sharply with its only other use in *Gatsby*, in the description of Myrtle's 'left breast . . . swinging loose like a flap', incapable of giving suck or sexual pleasure, after Gatsby's car has killed her (p. 131).

There is, however, another word in the novel which means 'breast' or 'nipple' – 'pap'; this occurs only once, but at a very significant moment: in Gatsby's vision of what he will renounce when he kisses Daisy for the first time – the chance to climb alone to the 'pap of life' and gulp 'the incomparable milk of wonder' (p. 107). If we link this 'pap' with the two uses of 'breast' in the novel, we have one of those complex patterns of imagery connecting different and sometimes widely separated parts of the novel which is characteristic of *Gatsby*: 'the fresh, green breast of the new world' can be seen as an earthly, territorial embodiment of 'the pap of life' but, like Myrtle's breast, its earthiness and seductiveness make it vulnerable; it can be ripped and torn. In the concluding passage of *Gatsby*, the sentence which immediately follows the phrase 'a fresh, green breast of the new world' indicates that this tearing has taken place: the trees which were once a feature of that 'breast' have 'vanished', but not by magic; they did not melt away like the inessential houses; human beings felled them. Nick's verb 'make way' is a decorous personification of the trees which implies that they politely made room for the newcomers; but the personification develops in a more sinister direction which suggests that the presumed innocence even of the new world is compromised: the trees 'pandered in whispers'. The verb 'pander' originally derived from the name Pandarus, a character in the medieval poem *Troilus and Criseyde* by Geoffrey Chaucer (*c*.1343–1400) who acts as a go-between to foster the love affair between his niece Cressida and Troilus; in that sense, the verb alludes to Nick's role in the affair between Gatsby and Daisy. It has since taken on the more general meaning of 'to gratify or indulge an immoral or distasteful desire or habit' and in this sense it suggests that the trees on 'the fresh green breast of the new world' appeal to dubious desires.

The sinister quality of this appeal is deepened by the phrase 'in whispers' which, in this context, especially recalls Marlow's comment on Kurtz in the novella which, as we said in the last chapter, influenced the structure of *Gatsby*: Conrad's *Heart of Darkness*: 'the wilderness . . . had whispered to him things about himself which he did not know, things of which he had no conception till he took counsel with this great solitude – and the whisper had proved irresistibly fascinating.' These sinister intimations cast a shadow over the phrase 'The last and greatest of all human dreams', though they do not wholly obscure its uplifting elements: the moment remains 'enchanted'. But it is also 'transitory', a fleeting moment in time, and the aesthetic contemplation it *compels* is neither understood nor wished for; it is the product of an intense but brief compulsion that will give way to actions – felling trees, felling indigenous inhabitants – which will transform the geographical and demographic shape of the continent. The moment is also subject to time because it is unrepeatable: it is happening for the last time in history.

In the second paragraph of the passage, Nick moves on to imply a similarity between those early dreamers and Gatsby. His dream, it is suggested, is also the dream of those Dutch sailors, of the early settlers. But he has come too late; the attempt to realize the dream has already been tried and has failed; the fields of the republic are 'dark' not only because it is night but also, and more significantly, because of the dark deeds which have taken place there – we may see another link here with Conrad's *Heart of Darkness*.

Insofar as the concluding paragraphs do refer to the American Dream and present Gatsby as representative of that dream, they reconfigure what has gone before in the novel and enable us to see it as offering a compressed history of America by means of metonymy – the rhetorical device in which a part stands for a larger whole, or vice versa – and anecdote. As with the story of Gatsby's life, these allusions are incomplete and fragmentary and are not presented in chronological order; the reader who wants to understand more about the novel's representation of America, like the reader who wants to understand more about Gatsby (and in practice, these will often be the same reader), has to extract the fragments, relate them where possible to the larger events and elements which they represent, and reassemble them in chronological order.

The end of the novel returns to the European occupation of American territory which laid the ground for the emergence of the USA, and it would thus feature first in such a reassembly. Next would come the description of the Buchanan mansion as 'Georgian Colonial', which alludes to the period in which America was a British colony under the rule of the English Kings George I, II and III – and it was during the reign of George III that the American Revolution against English rule took place (1775–83), the American Declaration of Independence was signed (1776) and the USA became a nation in its own right. The third fragment would be Nick's brief mention of the American Civil War (1861–5), which tore the USA apart and resulted in huge loss of life; however, Nick's great-uncle, who started the wholesale hardware business Nick's father still runs, evaded military service by hiring a substitute to go to war for him – which could be done for about $300. The fourth fragment would be that concerning Dan Cody, who, since he was 50 years old when Gatsby first met him in about 1907, would have been born about 1857. He is a tough man who has joined in all the hunts for precious metals that took place in the USA in the last quarter of the nineteenth century, including the rush for silver in Nevada, in the west, and for gold in the Yukon, in the north; he has made millions by trading in Montana copper; he is, in Nick's judgement, 'the pioneer debauchee, who during one phase of American life brought back to the Eastern seaboard the savage violence of the frontier brothel and saloon' (p. 97). He shares his forename with Daniel

Boone (1734–1820), the pioneer who founded the first settlement in Kentucky in 1775 and who became a legend in his own
lifetime, and his surname with William F. Cody (1846–1917),
known as 'Buffalo Bill', who popularized the Wild West show
and thus contributed significantly to the transformation of 'the
American West' into myth and spectacle – a process which
would be accelerated and greatly expanded by the development
of the movies. Cody is a transitional figure between the original
American pioneers like Boone and the big-time capitalists of
the early-twentieth-century USA who will convert the images of
those pioneers into powerful propaganda. But his own mental
faculties are failing and he is dominated and manipulated by a
woman, Ella Kaye, who sends him off on a yacht in 1902 and
who, when she comes on board ten years afterwards, seems to
precipitate or even perpetrate his death: Cody dies a week later.
Nick compares Kaye's role in relation to Cody to that of
Madame de Maintenon (1635–1719), the second wife of King
Louis XIV of France, who had a large and suspect influence
over her husband. In about the same year that Cody died, 1912,
a brewer built the house that would later be Gatsby's; he
intended to found a family and it was said that he had offered
to pay five years' taxes on all the cottages around him if their
owners would have their roofs thatched with straw, but they
refused and he went into a decline and died. The attempt to con-
struct a kind of tradition for oneself, to create a history, is
evident here. The final fragment is Nick's participation in the
First World War, which he briefly mentions near the start of the
novel, and which becomes the initial topic of conversation
between Nick and Gatsby before Nick realizes who Gatsby is.

So the range of historical reference in *Gatsby* spans the
European discovery of America, the colonial period, the US
Civil War, the hunt for mineral wealth in the last quarter of the
nineteenth century, and US involvement in the First World War.
The American history which can be reconstructed from the novel
raises challenging questions about the American Dream in the
past; those questions are amplified and developed by *Gatsby*'s
exploration of the American present of the 1920s. We shall now
examine this.

AMERICA: THE 1920s

(See discussion of Berman, Forrey, Hindus and Westbrook in Chapter 4, and 'America: The 1920s' section of Chapter 6.)

In *Gatsby* the present is, like the eponymous hero of the novel, an ambiguous, morally and politically questionable realization of the American Dream. It is a time characterized by vast wealth which is poured upon some and denied to others – compare Tom Buchanan and George Wilson; it is a time in which the old social elite, insofar as they are embodied in Tom Buchanan, are undisciplined, irresponsible, racist, idle and philandering; it is a time of violence. The kind of frontier savagery Dan Cody represents may have been 'forgotten' (p. 157), but the re-emergence of violence in the USA in the 1920s seems to suggest that it is an unavoidable element of American history and the American Dream: the rapt wonderment of the first Europeans who arrived in the new world quickly gave way to their violent settlement of the land, and the repression and expulsion of its indigenous inhabitants; the English and French colonial powers fought over the possession of territory and, when England emerged triumphant, it was soon trying to hold the American colonies by violence, only to be overthrown by violence; the US Civil War was a huge internecine conflict which claimed millions of lives; the rush for metals brought violence back to the East Coast of America; the First World War found America drawn into a European conflict for the first time. In the 1920s, violence is most apparent in the activities of gangsters – Gatsby sometimes looks as if he has killed a man, Rosy Rosenthal is shot three times in the belly – and it is also evident in the way in which Tom Buchanan treats women.

The American present in *Gatsby* is also a time in which explicit and implicit racist attitudes and practices prevail, and this raises the issue of the inclusiveness of the American Dream. Tom, the embodiment of American old money, is openly racist in his stumbling assertion that the white race is the dominant one which has produced science and art and all the elements of civilization, but which is now threatened by the rise of the coloured empires (p. 18). Nick does not endorse Tom's ideas in this respect but he does not directly condemn them either, seeing them as an index of Tom's intellectual backwardness rather than as an example of race prejudice: limited intelligence and intellectually outmoded ideas rather than racism; and Nick himself, a white Anglo-Saxon Protestant, displays a deprecatory attitude to members of ethnic groups other than his own. The Dutch sailors are sufficiently distant for him to see them as representative of 'man'; but members of contemporary ethnic groups other than his own are rarely seen or heard. His Finnish housekeeper is presented as a partly comic, partly disturbing figure who seems crucial to the running of his domestic life and who at one point provides useful information about Gatsby, but who is otherwise marginal, endowed with neither an articulate voice of her own nor a name – a striking omission, in this novel with so many names. In Chapter 1, Nick tells us that she mutters 'Finnish wisdom' when she is cooking (p. 9) and in Chapter 7, he provides us, in indirect speech, with her report on Gatsby's dismissal of his servants and its aftermath; but she never says a word in direct speech or has even a brief scene in which she and Nick engage in dialogue. Nick gives no sign that he has any conception that she has a life of her own and seems to think that she is at his beck and call – on the day of Gatsby and Daisy's visit to his bungalow, he recalls that he has forgotten to tell 'my Finn' to come back and goes to find her in what is presumably a poor quarter of West Egg, without any apparent awareness that she may have other demands on her time. Soon afterwards, she is the object of Gatsby's slightly reproachful look when Nick takes him into his pantry, and a little later her floor-shaking 'Finnish tread' alarms him (p. 82); when she brings in a tea tray for Gatsby and Daisy, Nick calls her 'the demoniac Finn' (p. 84). This deprecatory attitude towards a person of Scandinavian origin is echoed in a more general way by Nick's exclusion, in Chapter 9, of 'the lost Swede towns' from his idea of the Middle West (p. 167). Are Scandinavians also excluded from his idea of America?

Figures from other ethnic groups also remain on the periphery of Nick's consciousness and vision. In Chapter 2, he and Tom wait for the train to New York in the valley of ashes. It is a few days before the Fourth of July and Nick observes a grey, thin Italian child laying 'torpedoes' (firecrackers) along the railroad track which will explode when the train runs over them (p. 29). This probably underfed child, playing in a desolate, polluted environment, could seem an ironic comment on the celebration of America which takes place on the Fourth of July. On his drive with Gatsby into New York, Nick undergoes greater exposure to the gaze of ethnic otherness, although he is safely insulated from any contact that goes beyond the visual: the mourners in the cars which follow a hearse look out at Gatsby's spectacular vehicle 'with the tragic eyes and short upper lips of south-eastern Europe'; a limousine passes with a white chauffeur at the wheel and three fashionably dressed African-American passengers, two men and a girl; Nick laughs aloud as 'the yolks of their eyeballs rolled toward us in haughty rivalry' (p. 67). The racist stereotyping in which Nick momentarily engages when he sees the African-Americans is let loose when he meets Wolfshiem, a 'small, flat-nosed Jew' with 'two fine growths of hair' in his nostrils, 'tiny eyes' (p. 68) and 'Finest specimens of human molars' for cufflinks (p. 70). The novel itself does not imply that there is anything wrong with Nick's responses, but the modern reader may find the attitudes which he exemplifies questionable and see them as casting further doubt not only on the generosity and accuracy of Nick's perceptions, but also on the validity of the American Dream. Only Michaelis, the young Greek who runs the all-night restaurant and coffee house beside the ashheaps, is characterized in an extended and positive way, in the scene in Chapter 8 in which he stays with Wilson all night and tries to calm and console him after Myrtle's death, invoking the traditional sources of comfort – children and church – which Wilson does not possess. But Michaelis, who seems both compassionate and intelligent, is trapped in the valley of ashes, even if he is still young enough to escape.

Gatsby also shows an American present which is still drawing on European models that are implicitly presumed to be superior. For example, the exterior of Gatsby's house looks as though it is trying to imitate a *Hôtel de Ville* – a French city hall or municipal building – in Normandy, and inside it is a museum of

European styles: it includes a neo-Gothic library, panelled in carved English oak and named after an Oxford college, which was 'probably transported complete from some ruin overseas' (p. 46); Marie Antoinette music-rooms and Restoration Salons; and a study which imitates the designs of the eighteenth-century Scottish architects Robert Adam (1728–92) and James Adam (1732–94). Myrtle's apartment mirrors in miniature the multiple mimicries of Gatsby's mansion. It is crammed with overlarge furniture whose tapestry covers display scenes that come from or resemble those of eighteenth-century French rococo paintings, especially *The Swing* (about 1766, now in the Wallace Collection, London) by Jean-Honoré Fragonard (1732–1806). The implication is that Myrtle and Gatsby, both of humble origins, both in their respective ways romantics, and both representative of strands of populist vitality in American life, have in common a lack of taste and originality which especially shows itself in subservience to European stylistic models that are improperly understood. But it is not only Gatsby and Myrtle who are guilty of this: Tom, the embodiment of old money, endorses their lack of taste and originality, implicitly by paying for Myrtle's flat and furniture, and explicitly by becoming a kind of mimic man whose attempts to imitate the old colonizers through his riding clothes and his conversion of his garage into a stable threaten to turn him into an inadvertent parody of an English country gentleman.

It is important, however, to recognize that *Gatsby*'s portrayal of the American present is not wholly critical: the novel also conveys the excitement and appeal of modern America and thus foreshadows a world in which the American Dream will go global, not only because of the capacity of the USA to impose its will through violence, but also because of its ability to arouse, direct and gratify desire. Gatsby's parties may have their motivation in his desire to attract Daisy, but their extravagant conspicuous consumption also functions as an image of the USA itself: they depend, as Nick recognizes, on the toil of large squads of servants who clean, repair, prune and press buttons on kitchen gadgets: but these rude mechanicals disappear in the excitement, the exhilaration of the parties themselves – the cocktails come in 'floating rounds' as if by magic. Nick's account captures this excitement:

> The lights grow brighter as the earth lurches away from the sun, and now the orchestra is playing yellow cocktail music, and the opera of voices pitches a key higher. Laughter is easier minute by minute, spilled with prodigality, tipped out at a cheerful word. The groups change more swiftly, swell with new arrivals, dissolve and form in the same breath; already there are wanderers, confident girls who weave here and there among the stouter and more stable, become for a sharp, joyous moment the centre of a group, and then, excited with triumph, glide on through the sea-change of faces and voices and colour under the constantly changing light. (p. 42)

The first significant point about this passage is that it is mostly in the present tense throughout: 'grow', 'lurches', 'is', 'pitches', 'change', 'swell', 'dissolve', 'form', 'are', 'weave', 'become', 'glide'. Like most novels, *Gatsby* is told largely in the past tense, and this particularly befits its ostensible nature as Nick's retrospective account of his experiences; but the switch into the present tense at this point gives his account of Gatsby's parties a greater immediacy. The immediacy is more striking if we consider that this passage describes not one particular Gatsby party, but a typical Gatsby party, a synthesis of distinctive features drawn from Nick's observations of a number of parties that take place at his neighbour's mansion. If we recall the context of the passage, we will remember that it is the second of three present-tense paragraphs near the start of Chapter 3, and that this chapter opens with a description of Gatsby's parties as repeated events which is, though full of vivid detail, necessarily more distanced than an evocation of one particular party; to use the distinction we discussed in the previous chapter, it is more like 'telling' than 'showing'. The switch to the present tense, however, transfers us into the showing mode so vibrantly that the reader may well feel he or she is reading about a specific rather than a typical party, even though Nick does not start to describe a specific party – the first party that he goes to, where he meets Gatsby for the first time – until after the end of the third present-tense paragraph, when he shifts back into the past tense.

The next significant point is that the clause 'The earth lurches away from the sun' is an unusual way of describing the onset of evening; it reverses the imagery that is still in common use today, in which it is the sun rather than the earth which moves – 'sets' – as the day ends; an imagery that depends on a long-discredited pre-Copernican cosmology. Fitzgerald inverts this imagery and updates it to accord with a modern sense of the nature of the universe. But in doing so he also reanimates the kind of analogy between cosmic and human processes which occurs in Shakespeare and in the seventeenth-century Metaphysical poets, most notably John Donne (*c*.1572–1631): the change in the position of the earth in relation to the sun mirrors, on a much magnified scale, the change in human behaviour in relation to daylight standards of conduct which takes place at Gatsby's parties as night falls. Something of the nature of this change is suggested by one of those unusual combinations of words that are characteristic of the style of *Gatsby*: the juxtaposition of 'earth' and 'lurches'. 'Lurch' means 'to make a sudden, unsteady movement, to stagger', and it is an unexpected, rather undignified verb to apply to the earth; it offers an image of the transition from day to evening as a clumsy, erratic, abrupt shift rather than as a gentle gradation – as in the eighteenth-century 'Ode to Evening' by William Collins (1721–59) – or a magnificent pageant – as in the painting *The Fighting Téméraire* (1838) by the nineteenth-century Romantic painter J. M. W. Turner (1775–1851); it is, in other words, a Modernist, jarring way of describing the coming of night, and it matches the way in which some of the guests at Gatsby's party are starting to lurch with the intoxication of the alcohol and excitement.

A further unusual combination of words follows: 'yellow cocktail music'. 'Yellow' is one of the key colour adjectives in *Gatsby*, but its application to 'cocktail music' is an example of synaesthesia, in which experiences and perceptions that are usually associated with one of the five senses are transferred to another; in this example, sound (music) is expressed in terms of sight (yellow); this gives a sense of how daylight categories are starting to collapse and exchange qualities as the party gets under way. This blurring of categories is also suggested by the metaphor of 'the opera of voices'; this creates a kind of crossover effect, linking the popular cultural form of 'cocktail music' – light and frivolous music appropriate to the taking of cocktails in the evening – to the high-cultural form of opera, and transforming the fragments of party chit-chat into a dignified artistic production. The phrase 'opera of voices' also exemplifies the way in which individual human agents are displaced in this passage: the subjects of the verbs are not 'I', 'she' and 'he', but technological devices ('lights'), astronomical bodies ('earth', 'sun'), collective entities ('the opera of voices', 'the orchestra', 'groups') and generic forms of behaviour and types ('laughter', 'wanderers', 'girls'); human beings here are not unified and autonomous selves but are represented by metonymies. Metonymy is a figure of speech in which something is represented by a part of itself or by something closely associated with it; in this passage, however, parts which stand for human wholes almost come to substitute for or replace wholes: voices, laughter, faces become more important than specific individuals with distinctive features who might be talking or laughing. This foregrounding of part over whole gives a sense of processes in which people are caught up willy-nilly and, these processes, we could suggest, are not only those of Gatsby's parties but also of modern America and, given America's global reach, of the modern world. They are processes which displace individual identity and give a sense that everything is always changing, and fast.

This sense of rapid change is conveyed by some of the verbs we have already cited – 'swell', 'change', 'dissolve', 'form' – and by the sense that these processes are proceeding simultaneously, 'in the same breath', in an instant of human existence. Such change is exciting and in some ways liberating: for example, it provides the possibility of greater freedom for women, as the wandering girls who weave confidently about demonstrate. It may also be more deeply transformative, as the use of the term 'sea-change' in the last sentence of the passage suggests. The term originally comes from Shakespeare's play *The Tempest* (1611), where the spirit Ariel sings a song that seems to confirm

Ferdinand's mistaken belief that his father has drowned in the storm and that his corpse 'doth suffer a sea-change / Into something rich and strange' (1.2, 403–4); a more immediate intertext for its use in *Gatsby* is Eliot's *The Waste Land* which uses another line from Ariel's song (1.2.401) to suggest the ambivalent results of that transformation – 'Those are pearls that were his eyes' (l. 125) – and whose fourth section is called 'Death by Water'. In this *Gatsby* passage, the term 'sea-change' conveys the idea that the party, like modern America, can effect an apparently magical transformation but it also implies that such a change may be intimately connected with death; relating this idea to the eponymous

ansit to: WE-WK
em ID: 0000618588669
ll number: 813 FIT
tle: FITZGERALD'S THE GREAT GATSBY
thor: Tredell, Nicolas
ansit library: EU-MAIN
ansit reason: HOLD

[hero of the novel, it alludes to the transf]ormation that James [Gatz has already undergone through his] seagoing with Dan [Cody and that Jay Gatsby will undergo a]s he suffers his own [death by water, in the vulnerable luxury o]f his swimming pool, [...of the novel.]

[...on Gatsby's death is to return to] an awareness that the [...al transforma]tions which Gatsby's [...and symbolize are bound up], like the USA itself, [...and with a further great t]heme of Fitzgerald's [...we shall look at in the next se]ction of this chapter:

[MONEY]

[(See discussion of Godden in Chapter 4, an]d 'Money' section of Chapter 6.)

Gatsby is full of money. The novel allows its readers and critics – the majority of whom will not be millionaires – to be guests at Gatsby's parties, to live vicariously, as Nick does, in a world of fabulous wealth even as it implicitly, and sometimes explicitly, criticizes the moral and artistic shortcomings of that world. *Gatsby* challenges any simple opposition between money and happiness, material and spiritual wealth, money obtained by crime and money obtained by ostensibly legal means. In this novel, money is sexy, in both the erotic and the more generally exciting sense; it gives the kind of buzz that it would give again in the heady financial sprees of the 1980s. But it is also one of the most romantic and mysterious elements in the novel. Money may corrupt, but it also creates: it is crucial to Gatsby's attempt to realize his dream – he cannot take Daisy from Tom with money, but without money he could not even have tried to take her from him; it is crucial to the American Dream; and it is crucial to the twenty-first-century dream of global capitalism. All the major characters, perhaps all the minor ones as well, in the novel are significantly defined by their relationship to money. Money is not seen as external to some implied human essence but as shaping the ways in which people are perceived and the ways in which they perceive themselves, and the ways in which they behave. In Daisy's case, money permeates one of the most traditional channels of presence, individuality and authenticity: the voice.

Nick's great-uncle, the founder of his line, chose business, the making of money, over a war – the US Civil War – which was, in the view of some historians, itself motivated more by economic considerations than ethical ones – the struggle of the industrial North with the agricultural South mattered much more than slavery. Great-uncle Carraway was able to make that choice because he had the money to pay for a substitute to go to war in his place. In contrast to his prudent forebear, Nick has been to war and enjoyed it; but it has, at least temporarily, unfitted him for the family wholesale hardware business. The proceeds of that family business, channelled through his father, will, however, subsidize his attempt to change his relationship to money by becoming a financier rather than a wholesaler, selling bonds rather than hardware.

The term 'bond' is a significant one in relation to *Gatsby*'s exploration of the theme of money. It is word which suggests reliability and security: on the financial level, it is a certificate which a government or public company issues to a purchaser in which they promise to repay the value of the bond – its purchase price – at a fixed rate of interest at a specific time; while it may offer less of a return on an investment than shares, it provides greater security. On the social level, it also suggests the bonds which bind individuals together; Nick says that all his contemporaries are working in bonds, and there is an implication that in modern America financial bonds provide a means of human bonding, of creating some kind of like-minded community, in an epoch when other forms of bonding, other connections, have broken down. In the nineteenth century, the Scottish social thinker and writer Thomas Carlyle (1795–1881) observed in his book *Chartism* (1839) that, as a result of the changes brought about by industrial capitalism, 'cash payment has become the sole nexus [connection] between man and man'; by Fitzgerald's time, cash payment was increasingly being supplemented by other forms of payment, such as bonds, which were substitutes for money itself and which were making money increasingly intangible. The only times when physical money changes hands in the novel are the humble transactions between Tom and the dog seller in Chapter 2 ($10 for the 'Airedale') and Tom and Wilson in Chapter 8 ($1.20 for the gasoline). But the power of financial bonds to promote human community and dependability is shown to be limited in *Gatsby*: as an honest bond salesman, Nick does not make much money, as he admits to Gatsby, and Nick recognizes that he might, but for politeness, have been tempted in different circumstances to accept Gatsby's offer to help him make more, presumably by illegal means; near the end of the novel, when Nick answers the telephone to a caller who thinks Nick is Gatsby, he learns that Gatsby was involved in trading stolen bonds. In *Gatsby*, bonds, financial and human, are implicated in activities which deepen the mistrust between human beings.

In Chapter 3 of the novel, Nick portrays his hourly study of investments in the Yale Club library after his evening meal as an act of duty which he conscientiously performs before giving himself over to the freedom and excitement of walking the city and engaging in erotic and romantic fantasy. This suggests a familiar division between dull money and bright life; but that division has already been challenged by the visual allure of the books about finance which he buys when he starts work as a bond salesman; these books seem attractive and appealing, sources of sensuous pleasure: red and gold, the colour of blood and sun, they themselves look like new-minted money and promise to reveal the bright secrets of Midas, Morgan and Maecenas. This trio, linked in an alliterative chain, encapsulate the mixed attitudes to money, not simply of Nick, but of the whole novel – and, it might be said, of Western civilization. Midas is the mythical king whose touch turned everything to gold, including food, and who therefore starved to death because he could find nothing to eat; he illustrates that the lust for lucre may be fatal. Morgan is John Pierpont Morgan (1837–1913), the financier who founded the Morgan banking corporation, reorganized and revived flagging railway companies, and funded consolidations like US Steel and General Electric; he shows that the quest for wealth can lead to worldly success and power. Maecenas is Gaius Maecenas (c.70–8 BC), a Roman diplomat and famous patron of literature and the arts who encouraged the great classical poets Virgil (70–19 BC), Propertius (c.50–c.16 BC) and Horace (65–8 BC): he demonstrates that money can foster high culture. These examples provide a spectrum of attitudes to wealth which complicate any simple opposition between money and other human goods.

Nick's complex attitudes to money are also evident in his view of Tom. On the one hand, he is in awe of his huge wealth, as he is in awe of his huge body; on the other hand, he sees Tom's money as possibly encouraging him, and Daisy, in their irresponsible behaviour because it provides a refuge into which they can retreat from the consequences of the damage they cause. In contrast to Gatsby, there is no reference to, or speculation on, the source of Tom's wealth, and perhaps that is a key difference between 'old' and 'new' money: 'old' money is the money that arouses few questions about its sources. Since Tom comes from Chicago, it is possible that his wealth, like that of the Warrens in *Tender is the Night*, derives from one of the big meat-packing companies which developed in that city in the later nineteenth century; Upton Sinclair (1878–1968) offered an explosive exposé of this industry from the viewpoint of its workers in his novel *The Jungle* (1906). But we do not know; Tom's money is, to use a phrase Nick later coins about the lucre on which New York was built, 'non-olfactory' (p. 67) – it does not smell.

Money as well as sex is one of the bonds between Tom and Myrtle. If he gives her the sensuous satisfaction that her husband cannot deliver, he also provides her with the pleasures that money can buy – the pleasures of consumption and possession which the USA has now made globally attractive. When Tom takes Nick into Wilson's garage to meet 'my girl', the first adjective Nick uses to describe its interior is an economic one – 'unprosperous' (p. 27) – and its lack of prosperity is immediately demonstrated by the only car visible in this business which aims to make money by buying and selling cars: this is a wrecked and dusty Ford, which contrasts with Gatsby's magnificent car which will appear later and also provides a wry comment on Henry Ford (1863–1947), the founder in 1903 of the Ford Motor Company, a much-vaunted American success story and a leading representative of US industry, prosperity and the production of cheap consumer goods – epitomized by the Ford Model T – for the mass market. Nick's romantic imagination wants to reject the interior of the garage as an illusion, a shadow, and he surmises that 'sumptuous and romantic apartments' lie above (p. 27); but the only sumptuous and romantic apartment he does find is a parody of his imagined dwelling, Myrtle's small, furniture-stuffed New York apartment. When Tom, Myrtle and Nick reach that apartment, Nick implicitly invites the reader to share his deprecation of her lack of taste and of the snobbery she affects; but the narrative also displays Nick's snobbery and enables the reader to understand, even to share, the pleasure she takes in her furnishings, décor and dresses, in the purchases she makes on her trip to the city – a copy of a scandal magazine and a movie magazine, cold cream and perfume, and a puppy – and in the list she wants to make of the things she still has to buy – a massage and a wave, a collar for the puppy, an ash-tray with a spring mechanism, and, for her mother's grave, a wreath with a black silk bow which will last all summer. She is an early practitioner of retail therapy and Tom's money buys her a certain measure of happiness, brief though it may be. But her consumerism also contributes to her death – it is Wilson's discovery of the costly leather and braided silver dog-leash that she has bought for the puppy which leads him to suspect that she has been having an affair and to lock her up.

Gatsby's relationship to money is especially interesting. When he waits for Daisy to come to Nick's cottage for their first reunion after almost five years, he looks 'with vacant eyes' through a copy of what is presumably one of Nick's books about money, *Economics: An Introduction for the General Reader* (first published in the USA in 1918), by the British economist Henry Clay (1883–1954). While Gatsby would presumably find it difficult to read any book in these circumstances, the fact that it is a book about economics which fails to engage his eyes might seem to illustrate a familiar romantic – and Romantic – commonplace: the irrelevance of money to love. But in *Gatsby*, money, or the lack of it, is fundamentally interwoven with love. One response to that interweaving might be to advocate – as Clay's *Economics* does – redistributing wealth for the benefit of all; but this is not Gatsby's way. It is not that Gatsby has no concern with economics or with the distribution of income, but rather that he has a different understanding of it from that which an egalitarian economist might provide, and it is summed up in the most famous line of dialogue in the novel. This occurs in Chapter 7, in a passage which particularly merits close reading. It relates an exchange between Nick and Gatsby as they wait outside the Buchanan house to go to New York after Daisy has, in front of Tom, effectively but indirectly told Gatsby that she loves him:

> 'She's got an indiscreet voice,' I remarked. 'It's full of—' I hesitated.
> 'Her voice is full of money,' he said suddenly.
> That was it. I'd never understood before. It was full of money – that was the inexhaustible charm that rose and fell in it, the jingle of it, the cymbals' song of it . . . High in a white palace the king's daughter, the golden girl . . . (p. 115)

We can see first of all that Nick's 'It's full of—' provides a further example of the rhetorical device we discussed in Chapter 2 – the device of aposiopesis, a sudden breaking-off of a sentence indicated by a dash. But then Gatsby, who for most of the novel stays silent, speaks evasively, or has his words paraphrased by Nick, supplies the missing word with unusual conviction, clarity and directness, not by simply adding it on to the end of Nick's unfinished sentence, but by incorporating it into a complete and concise sentence of his own: 'Her voice is full of money.' The juxtaposition of Daisy's voice and money remains startling – even if one has read *Gatsby* before – because the previous descriptions of that voice have been couched in a romantic and erotic vocabulary rather than a financial one; prior to this moment, Nick has found it variously thrilling, exciting, compelling, glowing, singing, exhilarating, fluctuating, feverish, warm, deathless, murmuring, husky, rhythmic and sweet, and Jordan – the only other person besides Nick and Gatsby who comments on Daisy's voice – associates it with 'amours'.

The bottom-line identification of money as the key quality of Daisy's voice gives Nick a shock of recognition and his assent to Gatsby's statement is immediate and terse: 'That was it. I'd never understood before.' The statement is then repeated in Nick's narrative prose almost verbatim, but quickly followed by the elaborate vocabulary and rhythmic phrasing which often feature in Nick's storytelling style. The rhythm of Nick's prose at this point revives the lyrical quality that 'full of money' has threatened to dissipate; the internal part-rhymes – 'jingle'/'cymbals'/'king' – may sound slightly discordant, reminding us of Gatsby's monetary metaphor (especially if we recall 'the jingle of money' in Fitzgerald's *Crack-Up* essay, quoted in Chapter 1 of this guide). But Nick's prose also distracts us from this discord. It does not wholly do so, however. Nick employs the kind of romantic vocabulary we discussed in Chapter 2, and the most immediate ancestor of the images here is nineteenth-century pre-Raphaelite poetry and painting – for example, the work of Dante Gabriel Rossetti (1828–82) and William Morris (1834–96); but the context in which that vocabulary is used and the juxtaposition of such terms with Gatsby's comment brings out an element that is largely absent from pre-Raphaelite verbal and visual discourse: the material element, the element of money. This is not to say, however, that the material element negates the romantic element, or that the two elements are absolutely distinct: the juxtaposition of the two elements suggests that money is the stuff that dreams are made on.

The passage also has echoes of the Bible and of Greek myth. 'Cymbals', as a plural, occurs eight times in the Old Testament, in the Authorized Version of the Bible, but its most famous occurrence is in the New Testament, as a singular, in St Paul's First Letter to the Corinthians, 13.1: 'Though I speak with the tongues of men and of angels, and have not charity, I am become as sounding brass or tinkling cymbal.' On one level, we could apply this quotation to Daisy, who, we might say, speaks with the tongue of an earthly angel, but who – in her attitude to Gatsby, at least – lacks charity. But the allusion may also implicitly challenge the value of charity, in both its biblical and modern secular senses: could charity of either kind really have much effect against the cymbals that symbolize the magic of money?

The imagery of the golden girl, the king's daughter, high in a white palace, plays an intriguing variation on the ancient Greek myth of Danaë, who was imprisoned in a bronze tower by her father Acrisius, King of Argos, because of a prophecy that her son would kill him; Zeus, however, turned himself into a shower of gold, entered her room, and made her pregnant with Perseus. In Nick's revision of the image, it is the girl herself who takes a golden form to allure the vulnerable male, Gatsby, even though she has already had a child with the man of godlike physique, Tom. This play with traditional gender roles brings us to a fifth key theme of *Gatsby*: sexuality and gender.

SEXUALITY AND GENDER

(See discussion of Fraser, Fryer, Korenman and Person in Chapter 4, and 'Sexuality and Gender' section of Chapter 6.)

Gatsby vividly dramatizes the shifting definitions of masculinity and femininity and the uncertain roles of men and women in a society in transition. Tom Buchanan embodies – and here the verb 'embodies' seems especially apt – a powerful patriarchy threatened by social change; Daisy seems to find little satisfaction in the traditional roles of wife and mother but has no real alternative to them; Jordan Baker is a financially independent woman and sporting celebrity living a peripatetic life but she is harshly criticized and eventually rejected by Nick; Myrtle is a lower-middle-class woman of great but stifled vitality; Wilson lacks key signs of conventional masculinity; Gatsby feels 'married' to Daisy but he tries to break up Tom's marriage; and Nick is a sexually ambiguous figure.

As all these issues are refracted through Nick, the primary narrator of the novel, it is worth focusing on the sexual ambiguity which emerges from the story that is attributed to him, while keeping in mind that the issue of his erotic orientation can never finally be settled because he is a fictional character, a product rather than source of the discourse which he supposedly writes, and that discourse, in characteristic Modernist fashion, leaves gaps and uncertainties that are never bridged or resolved.

First of all, we can ask what Nick looks like. His appearance is hardly described at all in *Gatsby* – Fitzgerald makes no use of the stock devices by which a first-person narrator can realistically provide a physical description of himself – for example, by looking in a mirror or at a photograph – but two potentially contradictory references to his appearance are significant in relation to his sexuality. In the early pages of the novel, he tells us that he is said to resemble the great-uncle whose 'rather hard-boiled' portrait hangs in his father's office (p. 8). 'Hard-boiled' has strong masculine connotations – one thinks particularly of the 'hard-boiled detective' who features in American thrillers of the period – but we have learned just before Nick makes this statement that this great-uncle avoided service in the US Civil War and possibly had no children of his own to carry on the business he founded (unless – could there be a hint of this? – he adulterously fathered Nick's father); thus, despite the 'hard-boiled' appearance of Nick's great-uncle, he lacks two of the conventional signs of masculinity. So the masculine inheritance suggested by the physical resemblance is itself a dubious one. The second reference to Nick's physical appearance is on his first visit to the Buchanans, when Daisy says three times that he reminds her of a rose (p. 19). Nick does not object to this description to Daisy, but he does at once deny it emphatically to the reader, in a way that might, taken with other hints in the novel, seem suspicious, and carry a hint of 'The lady doth protest too much, methinks' (*Hamlet*, 3.2, 219). In 1920s America, a man who looked like a rose would not smell sweet; he would seem too feminine and threaten traditional gender boundaries.

Nick is perhaps particularly sensitive to Daisy's suggestion in Tom Buchanan's house because, as Nick has already observed, Tom has a body that is powerful enough to outweigh the 'effeminate' aspect of his riding clothes and can barely be contained by them; it is a phallic body that fills and seems ready to burst out of his boots; it shows 'a great pack of muscle shifting' when his shoulder moves under his coat; it is 'capable of enormous leverage – a cruel body' (p. 12). Nick's response is a complex one, starting from a degree of pleasure in response to the 'effeminate' aspect of Tom's appearance, moving to an admiration of the way in which the feminine aspect is outweighed by Tom's physique, and culminating in an awed recognition of the power of that physique and an admiration of, fear of and perhaps desire for its potential cruelty.

If Daisy threatens to turn Nick into a rose, Myrtle threatens to turn him into a nullity in the scene in her apartment when, riled by her sister's claim that she was crazy about Wilson for a while, she cries that she was no more crazy about him than about the man to whom she points suddenly – Nick (p. 37). A disconcerting momentary identification between Nick and Wilson is set up and there is a more general implication that a sensuous woman like Myrtle could not possibly consider Nick an object of desire. It is also in Myrtle's apartment that Nick meets a male character who is explicitly described as 'feminine' – Chester McKee, the photographer whose wife is, among other things, 'handsome': the couple seem to have exchanged conventional gender characteristics. After Tom shatters Myrtle's nose, McKee leaves the apartment, and Nick, without offering any explanation for his action, follows him; we shall engage in a close reading of the passage which follows:

'Come to lunch some day,' he suggested, as we groaned down in the elevator.

'Where?'

'Anywhere.'

'Keep your hands off the lever,' snapped the elevator boy.

'I beg your pardon,' said Mr McKee with dignity, 'I didn't know I was touching it.'

'All right,' I agreed, 'I'll be glad to.'

... I was standing beside his bed and he was sitting up between the sheets, clad in his underwear, with a great portfolio in his hands.

'Beauty and the Beast ... Loneliness ... Old Grocery Horse ... Brook'n Bridge ...'

Then I was lying half asleep in the cold lower level of the Pennsylvania Station, staring at the morning *Tribune*, and waiting for the four o'clock train. (pp. 39–40)

Nick's response to McKee's invitation is delayed by the elevator boy's rebuke which suggests McKee's hands have strayed, inadvertently or by subconscious impulse, into contact with a forbidden lever. On the literal level, the lever is presumably one of the lift controls, but the dictionary definition of a lever – 'a projecting arm or handle that is moved to operate a mechanism' – also suggests that it could be interpreted in symbolic terms as an erect penis. McKee's apology to the elevator boy is immediately followed by Nick's 'All right ... I'll be glad to'. This is ostensibly a reply to McKee's invitation to lunch; but insofar as it can be read as a response to the elevator boy's rebuke and to McKee's apology, it suggests that Nick would be glad to 'touch the lever'.

The narrative then cuts, without any transitional passage, to a brief but vividly realized scene in which Nick and McKee are in a bedroom together, with no indication of how they got there; it is one of only two bedroom scenes in the novel, and a more intimate one than the scene between Daisy and Gatsby in Chapter 5, where Nick is present and where the closest Gatsby gets to undressing is showering his shirts over Daisy – though not the one he is wearing. By contrast, McKee is in bed, clad in his underwear (Nick's state of dress is not indicated), and touching not a lever, but 'a great portfolio' which he holds in his hands.

It is important to stress that there is no textual evidence that a sexual encounter takes place between Nick and Chester – though it is most unlikely that there would be any such evidence in an American novel of 1925 by an author who hoped for a

large readership and financial rewards; *Gatsby's* representation
of adulterous and extramarital *hetero*sexuality led the editor of
one magazine, *Liberty*, to refuse it for serial publication, and
other magazines may have turned it down for similar reasons;
explicit *homo*sexuality would have been quite beyond the pale.
But we do not need to suppose that the McKee scene implies
that a homosexual encounter does occur to acknowledge
that the situation is fraught with homoerotic possibilities and
innuendoes. In this context, it is worth noting that the term
'underwear' which is used here recurs only once in the novel, in
Chapter 8: during the argument which leads to Nick, Jordan,
Tom, Daisy and Gatsby taking the parlour of a Plaza Hotel
suite, Nick confides, with an unusual frankness which resembles
that of James Joyce in *Ulysses*, that his underwear 'kept climb-
ing like a damp snake' round his legs (p. 120). Like the elevator
lever and the great portfolio, that 'snake' lends itself to a phallic
interpretation, though in this last case it suggests a flaccid rather
than an erect penis – and thus perhaps hints that Nick's body is
anticipating Gatsby's unmanning by Tom in the confrontation
over Daisy.

If Nick lacks erectness in the run-up to the Plaza Hotel scene,
there is another figure who possesses it from her first appearance
in the novel – Jordan Baker. In contrast to the sensuous, smouldering, incorrigibly female flesh of Myrtle, Jordan – the one character in the novel whom Nick admits that he enjoys looking at –
is androgynous: slim, with small breasts and 'an erect carriage'
which she emphasizes 'by throwing her body backward at the
shoulders like a young cadet' (p. 16). It is this hermaphrodite
body which Nick himself will soon throw backward but will
finally throw over. He is uneasy about his relationship with a
young woman who looks like an 'erect' young man and whose
prowess at playing and allegedly cheating at golf proves that she
knows how to handle her balls; the unacknowledged reason for
his uneasiness may be that she seems too much like a man – just
as his decision to reject the girl back home to whom he had been
writing letters signed 'Love, Nick' seemed to relate to the mous-
tache of perspiration that appeared on her upper lip when she
played tennis and thus not only made her female fleshliness

sweatily apparent but also, and perhaps more disturbingly, turned her into a man.

Nick's attitude to Jordan contains considerable elements of hostility and patronizing indulgence which could be read as a defence against his attraction to her. Of the three major women characters in *Gatsby*, Jordan has departed furthest from conventional notions of femininity and might, in some emancipated perspectives, seem an admirable figure: she is single, financially independent and has a reputation of her own as a golf champion which seems to be based primarily on ability; Nick, by comparison, is Mr Nobody from Nowhere and he might be expected to think himself lucky to be the escort of a sports celebrity. He shows no sign of doing so, however, and it is perhaps useful to him that he can take the moral high ground in relation to her by labelling her a cheat. An incident in which, when they are together at a house party, she leaves a borrowed convertible out in the rain and lies about it, presumably to its owner, is, for him, confirmation of a story that she had moved her ball from a bad lie in her first big golf tournament: an act that echoes, on a smaller scale, the fixing of the baseball World Series which shocks Nick so much when Gatsby tells him that Wolfshiem was responsible for it. Despite Nick's claim at the start of the novel that he is 'inclined to reserve all judgements' (p. 7), he seems highly judgemental in the way he moves from a lie that he presumably witnesses or hears about – without apparently contradicting or protesting against it at the time or afterwards – to the assumption that the rumour that Jordan cheats at golf is true and then to the assertion that she is 'incurably dishonest'. He gives no further examples of her alleged dishonesty and there is no indication that, despite their intimacy, he tries to check out the truth of the cheating rumour with her, even indirectly. Instead he goes on to take her dishonesty for granted and to excuse her on the sexist ground that 'Dishonesty in a woman is a thing you never blame deeply (pp. 58–9)'. It seems clear, however, that he does blame her deeply – but perhaps less for dishonesty than for awakening his uneasy sexuality. The assumption of her dishonesty may be a projection of his own dishonesty about the sexual ambiguity in himself which his relationship with her has helped to highlight.

Myrtle Wilson is imbued with vitality – the adjective is applied to her four times, and only used on one other occasion in the novel, when Nick speaks of the 'colossal vitality' of Gatsby's illusion. When Nick first meets her, he at once sees a vitality which makes her seem as if 'the nerves of her body were continually smouldering' (p. 28); though dwelling in the valley of ashes, she smoulders with banked-up rather than dying fire. In her New York apartment, after she has changed her costume, her 'vitality' changes to quasi-aristocratic disdain but has returned when he later glimpses her, from Gatsby's car, 'straining at the garage pump with panting vitality' (p. 66) – an energetic, sexually suggestive image which contrasts with the inert image of her husband that Tom evokes when he mockingly suggests that Mr McKee should take a photograph of 'George B. Wilson at the Gasoline Pump' (p. 35). The final use of the word 'vitality' occurs in the description of her death when her wide-open mouth, 'ripped a little at the corners', looks 'as though she had choked a little in giving up the tremendous vitality she had stored so long' (p. 131).

Near the end of the novel, Daisy is harshly criticized by Nick and placed on the same level as Tom but her position is, to say the least, a difficult one. Marriage to the young Second Lieutenant Gatsby would present many problems, and when he meets her again, she is a wife and a mother, even if she is not happy or fulfilled in those roles, and Gatsby is involved in large-scale organized crime. The idea that they should go back and marry from her home in Louisville seems impractical and unreal – what would they do about Daisy and Tom's daughter, for example? Tom's rampant infidelities began soon after their marriage. Gatsby makes an impossible demand on her – that she deny that she ever loved Tom. In refusing to do this, Daisy displays an honesty that Nick, who affirms his own honesty, perhaps ought to admire. Daisy's decision to cover up the truth about Myrtle's death – and Gatsby's – is one to which Nick implicitly assents – he could, after all, have made a statement to the police and given evidence at the inquest.

In *Gatsby*, Fitzgerald portrays a range of possible roles and positions for women and for men and shows their constricting effects. Daisy and Myrtle are both, in their different ways, trapped, even though it is the lower-class Myrtle who is the sacrificial victim whose death restores the equilibrium of Tom and Daisy's relationship. Jordan is comparatively free, but is the object of harsh judgement and eventual rejection by Nick. Tom and Wilson are both, in their respective ways, trapped by patriarchal stereotypes, and both lash out violently to assert their power over the vital Myrtle. Nick is caught between gender positions, a hard-boiled rose, who has a bedroom scene with a feminine man and a half-loving relationship with a masculine woman. In its exploration of the theme of gender and sexuality, *Gatsby* shows that appearances can be deceptive and that truth seems contradictory, complex and hard, perhaps impossible; and in these respects, this theme, like the others which we have explored so far, links up with what may be the overarching theme of the novel: appearance and reality.

APPEARANCE AND REALITY

(See discussion of Berman and White in Chapter 4, and 'Appearance and Reality' section of Chapter 6.)

When Gatsby and Daisy meet again in Nick's bungalow after almost five years, Nick leaves them alone together, goes out into the garden, takes shelter under a tree from the pouring rain, and for half an hour stares at Gatsby's huge mansion 'like Kant at his church steeple' (p. 85). The reference at this point in the novel to the great German philosopher Immanuel Kant (1724–1804), who was supposed to have looked at a church steeple from his study window as he engaged in abstract thought, is, on one level, the knowing joke of a university-educated man with a superficial philosophical culture trying to provide himself, and his readers, with a moment of light relief in an emotionally tense and physically uncomfortable situation. But on another level, and taken in the context of *Gatsby* as a whole, the reference suggests that Nick is a kind of philosopher – not because he possesses the exceptional intellectual prowess of a thinker of genius such as Kant, but because he is constantly, anxiously engaged in trying to distinguish between appearance and reality. In a novel which dramatizes a range of philosophical positions – from Gatsby's Platonic idealism to Jordan Baker's universal scepticism – Nick's anxiety, his knack of getting into tangles, and his attempts to grasp, to represent and sometimes to analyse those situations through thinking and writing, make him an existentialist, seeking meaning in an apparently absurd world and basing his thought on specific situations, not on abstractions. Nick, like the novel which he supposedly writes, conducts his philosophical investigations through the techniques of art, of fiction – characters, scene, situation and symbolism.

In the previous chapter of this guide, we saw the importance of the symbolism of eyes in *Gatsby*; in considering the philosophical implications of the novel in this chapter, we can suggest that eyes, the most sophisticated of the human sense organs, are a metonym for the attempt to grasp reality through sense-impressions – sense-impressions which have to be processed by the understanding to make sense. Nick himself spends a lot of the novel looking and listening, and initiates action himself only rarely; most of the time, he appears to be tagging along for the ride, a restless eye/I trying to see what he can see and to understand it; and, despite the confidence of many of his general pronouncements, he, and the other characters whom we see through his eyes, often find seeing difficult. In *Gatsby*, the problem of accurate perception is sometimes significantly focused by accounts of the act of looking at a photograph or through windows. For example, when Nick first enters Myrtle's apartment – and this is before he has had anything to drink – he sees a photograph which seems to be a hen sitting on a blurred rock; looked at from a distance, however, the image resolves itself, like an Impressionist painting, and becomes a bonnet which tops the beaming face of a stout old lady; the more general implication is that appearances are deceptive and may change and vary in accuracy according to the distance from which one observes them. While Nick later identifies the lady in the enlarged photo as Myrtle Wilson's dead mother – one of only two mothers mentioned in the text, the other being Daisy – he nonetheless finds that it hovers like the ectoplasm which a spiritualist medium supposedly extrudes: here, the photograph becomes an ironic comment on the attempt to demonstrate the existence of life after death by visual means.

In *Gatsby*, looking through windows provides an especially important set of models of perception and misperception, of the desire and quest for knowledge and its satisfaction or frustration. Although Nick claims, near the start of the novel, that it is better to look at life through a single window, he himself looks through or at, or sees or imagines other people looking through or at, a range of windows. In the eyes of the casual watcher in the street below, as imagined by Nick, the windows of Myrtle's apartment awaken but do not satisfy the desire for knowledge. The poor young clerks whom Nick observes on his nocturnal wanderings through New York loiter in front of windows – presumably shop windows – which, we may infer, awaken the desire for the knowledge that comes with possession of the goods those windows display, and the lifestyles which they connote; but they also thwart those desires, which only money – or theft – can satisfy. The windshields in Gatsby's car seem like a maze of mirrors in their multiple reflections of the sunlight, while its layers of glass enclose its driver and passengers in a conservatory of green leather: here, an accumulation of windows seems to obstruct rather than assist perception and knowledge, like the windscreen of a car one drives in a nightmare which prevents one from seeing the road ahead properly. It is through the windows of the cars that pass Gatsby that Nick sees – or, more precisely, fails properly to see – people of south-east European origins and African Americans whom he instantly slots into his perceptual stereotypes; they, in turn, are looking at Gatsby's car, but their eyes – as yet – lack sufficient social power to make Nick feel that he himself is under scrutiny and to bounce his gaze back upon himself. It is through a window in Gatsby's bedroom that Daisy looks out at the pink and golden foamy clouds over the sea, a setting for a rococo version of the Birth of Venus, and says that she would like to push Gatsby around in one of them, suggesting her flimsy grasp of the reality of Gatsby or of her own situation. When Tom and Nick stop for gas at Wilson's garage on the fatal day which will climax in Myrtle's death, Nick glimpses, through a curtained window above the garage, not the romantic and sumptuous apartments which he had once imagined there, but Myrtle's face peering down; she does not see Nick, who is able to observe the emotions creeping into her face 'like objects into a slowly developing picture' (p. 119) and concludes that she is looking with 'jealous terror' on Jordan Baker, whom, Nick believes, she takes to be Tom's wife (it could also be that she takes Jordan to be Tom's new mistress and that Nick does not entertain this thought because it would highlight the fragility of his own hold upon Jordan and raise the possibility that a macho man like Tom could take her from him). After Myrtle's death, it is at the window of Daisy's room that Gatsby, on the outside of his dream girl's house once more, looks for a signal of distress – turning the light on and off – which will never come: this window will show him nothing; he is a priest whose God has absconded but who still waits for a sign. Meanwhile Nick looks through the gap between the pantry window curtain and the sill and sees Tom and Daisy sitting together at the kitchen table, appearing to be both intimate and conspiratorial – and believes he has understood the truth of the situation.

The image of the window also calls up the view of the German philosopher Gottfried Leibniz (1646–1716) in which the universe consists of 'windowless monads'. Nick is a monad with a window who constantly strives for a more panoptic view, a first-person storyteller who tries to become an omniscient narrator, a restless eye who is also a restless I, not content to stay within the limits of his own perception and knowledge; a narrator who asserts that it is better to look at life from one window but who tries, at especially significant moments, to look at life through the windows of other people's eyes and minds. At the end of Chapter 6, for example, when he imagines Gatsby kissing Daisy for the first time, he provides a far more complete, cohesive and convincing story than Gatsby himself could have supplied, if we judge by his own unconvincing account of himself to Nick in Chapter 4; and near the end of Chapter 8, Nick imagines, in a particularly powerful and convincing way, how Gatsby must have felt after the collapse of his dream of renewing the past with Daisy. What grounds does Nick have for his apparent knowledge of these events, of what Gatsby saw and felt? He employs, one presumes, a mixture of imagination that calls on his own fantasies and desires, and inference from his knowledge and experience of Gatsby and of Gatsby's situation; but at crucial moments he tries to present this mixture as if it were the authoritative discourse of an omniscient narrator. Inevitably, however, his authority is undermined by those elements of his style and stance which remind the reader that his viewpoint is the relativist one of the first-person narrator. So there is a fluctuation in the novel between an aspiration to absolute knowledge and an acknowledgment of the difficulty of attaining even the comparatively humble goal of accurate perception.

This fluctuation is not just the problem of Nick or of the novel in which he appears, however; it is a long-standing philosophical problem which becomes especially pressing in the modern world because the social and cultural structures – those of Christianity, for example – which placed limits on relativism are breaking down. The absence of absolute knowledge, the plunge into relativism, could seem liberating; perhaps it is for Jordan Baker, the representative in the novel of 'universal scepticism' (p. 77), the harbinger of jaunty postmodernism, for whom everything is permitted, even lying or cheating at golf. For Nick, however – and here he is joined by many other Modernist characters and artists – the plunge into relativism is a plunge into anguish, into distress and potential despair. One of world literature's great descriptions of such anguish occurs in *Gatsby* in the passage where Nick imagines what Gatsby must have felt like on the day of his death, when no telephone call comes from Daisy:

> I have an idea that Gatsby himself didn't believe it would come, and perhaps he no longer cared. If that was true he must have felt that he had lost the old warm world, paid a high price for living too long with a single dream. He must have looked up at an unfamiliar sky through frightening leaves and shivered as he found what a grotesque thing a rose is and how raw the sunlight was upon the scarcely created grass. A new world, material without being real, where poor ghosts, breathing dreams like air, drifted fortuitously about . . . like that ashen, fantastic figure gliding toward him through the amorphous trees. (pp. 153–4)

We can see how this passage begins with a speculative, provisional, conversational, almost casual sentence – 'I have an idea', 'perhaps'; the narrator invites the reader to join him in speculation but does so in an apparently humble way, acknowledging that it is a matter of an idea rather than of facts, of possibility rather than certainty. The next sentence starts in a more formal though still provisional conditional mode – '*If* that was true' – but then adopts a verb form which brings with it a more definite and insistent tone – 'he *must have* felt'. It is as if we were being led, gently but firmly, into accepting the narrator's version of things. As the sentence goes on, our interest is diverted from the provisional nature of the narrator's account by his exploration of what Gatsby *felt*: and the first element of Gatsby's feelings is a sense of loss. To convey what has been lost, the passage employs a phrase which, remarkably, combines nostalgic, sensuous and global connotations: 'the old warm world'; the implication is that he has lost the past – 'old'; that he has lost sensuous comfort – 'warm'; and that he has lost everything – 'the world'. The sentence then moves into an economic metaphor – 'paid a high price' – which has a bitterly ironic relation to the many references to money in the novel. In material terms, Gatsby has indeed paid a high price; but the psychic cost is so much greater. The sentence concludes with a precise diagnosis of the cause of Gatsby's current condition: he has lived too long with a single dream; but the phrasing here implies that the 'dream' can also be harmful, can turn into damaging obsession. The next sentence once more employs the 'must have' formula but this time the reader is likely to be so gripped by the evocation and analysis of Gatsby's state that he will not linger on its provisional, speculative nature but move quickly into the account of Gatsby's perceptions – and it is his perceptions, especially visual ones, which are in the forefront here. What he sees is the world of nature and horticulture: there are none of the signs of modernity which are visible through so much of the novel – cars, roads, petrol pumps, railways, the grey heaps of the valley of ashes and the white heaps of New York skyscrapers. All are absent and we are returned to the pre-urban, pre-industrial landscape of the early Romantic poets. But nature here brings no comfort; indeed, it is described in the kind of way which is more commonly associated with the negative experience of urban life, particularly when encountering the city for the first time; it is disorientating, alarming, chilling, ugly: the sky is 'unfamiliar', the leaves are 'frightening', a rose is 'grotesque' and the sunlight is 'raw': and it produces a reaction which is first of all physical: 'shivered'. The last phrase of the sentence takes up the idea of 'rawness' and sets it in a quasi-biblical context: the 'scarcely created grass' seems to evoke a primal moment, the moment just after God created the world, but this is a world from which God is absent and it needs the completion which only the human imagination can provide. But the human imagination, insofar as it is embodied in Jay Gatsby, has broken down.

The start of the final sentence of the passage abandons the 'must have' formula and indeed abandons the pronoun 'he': the narrator is no longer telling us what Gatsby must have felt – or what he himself feels – but presenting an omniscient summary of the nature of this strange new world – a new world which is very different, much more alien, than the new world whose 'fresh green breast', flowering for the Dutch sailors, reassuringly recalls the 'old warm world' of the mother. This new world is material rather than maternal; it lacks the reality which imagination can give; it is a world of the dead, of ghosts who feed on dreams which no longer have any possibility of realization, which can no longer animate reality. The implication is that Gatsby now belongs to that world, even though he is not yet physically dead. But he soon will be: the 'ghost' imagery which is used here was applied earlier in the novel to a man whose wife walked through him 'as if he were a ghost' (p. 28): George Wilson. After the pause provided by the ellipsis (the three dots) it is Wilson who will, so to speak, complete the sentence. Wilson is not named, but the adjectives 'ashen' and 'fantastic', following on from the 'ghost' imagery, help to identify him by associating him with the valley of ashes which is called 'fantastic' when it is first described at the start of Chapter 2. The verb 'gliding' both conveys the sense of a supernatural quality in Wilson's movements and suggests, on a realistic level, its silence, stealth and speed; the ineffectual Wilson at last proves himself lethally effective against a war veteran and gangster who could presumably, in other circumstances, have defended himself with ease. But, in a final twist of absurdity, Wilson has got the wrong man. In a sense, however, the death of Gatsby is merely the coda to the collapse of meaning that Nick so vividly evokes; and it is that collapse of meaning, the philosophical vacuum that it leaves, with which Nick will have to cope.

In the end – which is, of course, the beginning of the novel – Nick seems to have turned away from the urgent philosophical questions which his experiences at West Egg posed. He appears to have reduced his philosophical concerns to the question of how to regulate human behaviour and to have settled for an answer that combines a measure of the pragmatism of William James, which we discussed in Chapter 1 of this guide with a trace of the sort of authoritarianism which would, in certain contexts, harden in the next decade into fascism. Nick claims that he does not care about the philosophical foundations of conduct; these may be firm ('hard rock') or yielding ('wet marshes'), but beyond a certain point of licence, it seems to him necessary to maintain a kind of quasi-military discipline which, metaphorically, puts the world in uniform and makes it stand permanently at moral attention (p. 8). For Nick, however, this answer may be only temporary, like his loss of interest in the joy and sadness of human beings; after all, it is an answer he proffers as a preamble to a narrative which reopens all the questions he has supposedly shut down – reopens them not as abstract conundrums but as vivid existential challenges. And it is these challenges, above all, which give *Gatsby* its ongoing life.

DISCUSSION POINTS, QUESTIONS AND SUGGESTIONS FOR FURTHER STUDY

Romanticism

1. Read John Keats's 'Ode to a Nightingale' – you can also listen to a recording of Fitzgerald reading the poem at www.sc.edu/fitzgerald/voice.html. As well as the passages discussed earlier in this chapter, can you find other passages in *Gatsby* which seem to you to be imbued with a similar mood to Keats's 'Ode'?

2. In a notebook entry first published in *The Crack-Up*, Fitzgerald wrote 'Romanticism is really a childish throwback horror of being alone at the top – which is the real horror' (p. 148). What exactly does this definition mean, and how might it apply to *Gatsby*?

America: Dream and History

1. Shortly before publication, Fitzgerald tried unsuccessfully to change the title of *The Great Gatsby* to *Under the Red, White and Blue*, perhaps with reference to the national banners flying during the war which Jordan mentions in her account of Daisy in Louisville (p. 72). In what ways might this be a suitable title for the novel?
2. In the last-but-one paragraph of the novel, Fitzgerald uses the adjective 'orgastic'. When his editor, Maxwell Perkins, queried this, asking whether it should be 'orgiastic', Fitzgerald affirmed that 'orgastic' should remain in the text. What does this adjective mean and what does it contribute to the idea of the American Dream in the closing passages of the novel?

America: The 1920s

1. Reread the famous list of Gatsby's party guests at the start of Chapter 4 of the novel (pp. 60–2). What image of American society in the 1920s do these names give? What is Nick's attitude to that society? Is it possible to infer Fitzgerald's attitude?
2. Reread Nick's account of his evenings in New York in Chapter 3 of the novel, in the section which starts 'Reading over what I have written so far . . .' and ends 'Imagining that I, too, was hurrying toward gaiety and sharing their intimate excitement, I wished them well' (pp. 56–8). Then turn to the Modernist work that has often been linked with *Gatsby*, T. S. Eliot's *The Waste Land*, go to the third section of the poem, which is called 'The Fire Sermon', and read the account of a London evening which starts at line 215, 'At the violet hour, when the eyes and back' and ends at line 256, 'And puts a record on the gramophone'. Compare and contrast the attitudes to the modern city in these two accounts.

Money

1. The third paragraph of Fitzgerald's 17,000-word short story 'The Rich Boy' (1926) begins with a statement which has become famous: 'the very rich . . . are different from you and me.' Often, however, the rest of the paragraph is not quoted. Find a copy of the story (see Chapter 6 of this guide for details of where you can do this) and read the complete paragraph (the whole story is also well worth reading, both in itself and in relation to *Gatsby*). How do you think the paragraph's remarks about the very rich might apply to the representation of the rich in *Gatsby*?

2. Fitzgerald's remark about the 'very rich' provoked an equally famous riposte from Ernest Hemingway in 'The Snows of Kilimanjaro': 'Julian . . . had started a story once that began, "The very rich are different from you and me." And . . . someone had said to Julian, Yes, they have more money' (pp. 65–6). How far does *Gatsby* confirm or contradict the view that the only difference between the very rich and other people is that the very rich have more money?

Sexuality and Gender

1. In a newspaper clipping pasted in his scrapbook, and reproduced in *The Romantic Egoists* (1974), Fitzgerald is quoted as saying that the Midwest girl is 'unattractive, selfish, snobbish, egotistical [and] utterly graceless' (p. 97). In *Gatsby*, Daisy and Jordan Baker are clearly identified as Midwest girls, and the Midwest sometimes seems to be the place of virtue in the novel. How far does Fitzgerald's description fit Daisy and Jordan?

2. In a notebook entry first published in *The Crack-Up*, Fitzgerald wrote: 'Fifty years ago we Americans substituted melodrama for tragedy, violence for dignity under suffering. That became a quality that only women were supposed to exhibit in life or fiction – so much so that there are few novels or biographies in which the American male, tangled in an irreconcilable series of contradictions, is considered as anything but an unresourceful and cowardly weakwad' (*The Crack-Up*, p. 208). How far does this description of 'the

American male' in fiction and biography accord with the representations of the major male characters in *Gatsby*?

Appearance and Reality

1. Fitzgerald has been called 'a romantic philosopher caught in his own trap'. On the basis of *Gatsby*, what do you think this philosophical 'trap' might be and how far is it true that Fitzgerald was 'caught' in it?

2. Read section 5, 'What the Thunder Said', of Eliot's *The Waste Land* and pay particular attention to lines 411–14: 'I have heard the key / Turn in the door and turn once only / We think of the key, each in his prison / Thinking of the key, each confirms a prison.' Eliot's note to these lines quotes from *Appearance and Reality* (1893) by the philosopher F. H. Bradley (1846–1924): 'My external sensations are no less private to myself than are my thoughts or feelings. In either case my experience falls within my own circle, a circle closed on the outside; and, with all its elements alike, every sphere is opaque to the others which surround it . . . In brief, regarded as an existence which appears in a soul, the whole world for each is peculiar and private to that soul.' To what extent does *Gatsby* portray characters (including Nick) who are 'opaque' to one another, closed within their own spheres, and what are the philosophical implications of this?

CHAPTER 4

CRITICAL RECEPTION AND PUBLISHING HISTORY

CRITICAL RECEPTION

Gatsby received a mixed critical reception on its first appearance in 1925. The spectrum of responses can be summed up by two contrasting review headings: the *New York World* (12 April 1925) declared that the book was a 'dud', while the *Chicago Daily Tribune* (18 April 1925) affirmed that the novel proved that Fitzgerald was 'really a writer'. Several reviewers felt that *Gatsby* was more mature than *This Side of Paradise* and *The Beautiful and Damned*; for example, William Curtis, in *Town and Country* (15 May 1925), said that meeting Fitzgerald again in *Gatsby* after encountering him in his two previous novels was like 'realizing that a hopeful child has become adult', while Gretchen Moult roundly affirmed in the *Detroit Free Press* (21 June 1925): 'Scott Fitzgerald has grown up.' *Gatsby*'s technique also came in for praise. Walter K. Schwinn, for example, in a clipping in Fitzgerald's scrapbook whose source has not been identified, commended 'the masterly organization of the narrative', and an anonymous review that Fitzgerald also pasted into his scrapbook identified two aspects of the novel which would receive much attention from later critics: the way in which the reader's knowledge of Gatsby is built up piecemeal by means of what Nick hears and sees, and the motif of the eyes of Dr T. J. Eckleburg.

The reviews made a range of comparisons with other writers, most often Henry James: for instance, Edwin Clark, in the *New York Times Book Review* (19 April 1925) likened *Gatsby* to Henry

James's *The Turn of the Screw* (1898) in terms of its shortness and its refusal to resolve crucial uncertainties; Carl van Vechten, in *The Nation* (20 May 1925), suggested that *Gatsby* and James's *Daisy Miller* (1879) shared the theme of 'a soiled or rather cheap personality transfigured and rendered pathetically appealing through the possession of a passionate idealism'; and Gilbert Seldes in *The Dial* (August 1925) remarked that Fitzgerald had got the novel's 'scenic method' from James via Edith Wharton. In the *New York World*, Laurence Stallings compared *Gatsby* to the work of another writer whom Fitzgerald acknowledged as an influence: Willa Cather. Stallings felt that Cather's *A Lost Lady* and *Gatsby* both combined a mature viewpoint and a central character who lacked depth.

As well as the review response to *Gatsby*, another significant aspect of its contemporary reception comprised the letters of praise that Fitzgerald received from writers whom he admired. One of these came from Cather, and another from the author whose influence on *Gatsby* Seldes had detected: Edith Wharton. While Wharton commended the 'seedy orgy' at Myrtle's apartment and the characterization of Wilson and Wolfshiem (though her remarks on the latter sound anti-Semitic today), she felt that Fitzgerald would have increased the impact of Gatsby's downfall if he had presented a fuller picture of his earlier career; she acknowledged, however, that this would have been an old-fashioned way to do it, which was not Fitzgerald's way. The highly experimental Modernist writer Gertrude Stein (1874–1946), however, made a comparison that might have seemed to make Fitzgerald look very old-fashioned in early-twentieth-century terms when she told him he was 'creating the contemporary world' in much the same way that the Victorian writer William Makepeace Thackeray (1811–63) did in his novels *Vanity Fair* (1847–8) and *The History of Pendennis* (1848–50). But Fitzgerald, who much admired Thackeray, took this as a compliment, and Stein's comment was insightful in that it recognized the extent to which *Gatsby* was not simply *reflecting* 1920s America but creatively *constructing* a version of it which, nearly a century later, continues to shape our perceptions of that decade. T. S. Eliot, in his letter from England, said that he had read the novel three times and that it had 'interested and excited' him more than any new English or American novel he had seen for some years; he told Fitzgerald that he would like to write to him more fully when he had time and explain exactly why it seemed to him such a remarkable book, 'the first step that American fiction has taken since Henry James'. Eliot appears never to have provided a full explanation of his reasons for admiring *Gatsby*, however, and his analysis of the novel remains one of the most tantalizing pieces of unwritten criticism of the twentieth century. But the comments he did make provided excellent copy for future paperback editions of the novel.

Like its American counterpart, the first British edition of *Gatsby*, in 1926, had a mixed response from reviewers. T. S. Eliot acted as a kind of US ambassador in England for the novel, commissioning two reviews for his magazine *The Criterion* from American writers. Gilbert Seldes, who had already reviewed the book in the USA, praised the book again in the January 1926 issue, while in the October 1926 issue the American poet, novelist and short-story writer Conrad Aiken (1889–1973) applauded *Gatsby*'s formal excellence and, like Seldes, van Vechten and Clark, suggested Henry James as a possible influence, particularly 'the flash-backs and close-ups and parallel themes' of *The Awkward Age* (1889). Aiken's use of cinematic terms, however, indicates what he saw as the primary influence on *Gatsby*: film. The anonymous review in the *Times Literary Supplement* (18 February 1926) praised Fitzgerald's novel as an undoubted work of art 'of great promise' – though this last phrase implies 'could do better' – and made a significant comparison not with Henry James, the favoured choice of reviewers so far, but with a writer who would come to loom much larger than James in later critical considerations of Fitzgerald: Joseph Conrad. It saw Gatsby as 'a Conradian hero' like the eponymous protagonist of *Almayer's Folly* (1895) or 'the hero' – presumably Kurtz – of *Heart of Darkness* (1902). This suggested a depth in *Gatsby* which the writer L. P. Hartley (1895–1972) did not perceive. In *The Saturday Review*, he took the novel as an example of 'an unmistakable talent unashamed of making itself a motley to the view' (that is, making a fool of itself) and dismissed the story as 'absurd'.

In its first French translation, *Gatsby le magnifique* (1926), Fitzgerald's novel received a splendid though belated endorsement from the well-known writer and artist (and later film director) Jean Cocteau (1889–1963). In a 1928 letter to the translator Victor Llona, which Llona passed on to Fitzgerald, Cocteau called *Gatsby le magnifique* 'un livre *céleste*: chose la plus rare du monde' ('a *heavenly* book: the rarest thing in the world'). Llona remarked to Fitzgerald, however, that it was too bad that Cocteau had not written this in the papers when the translation came out in 1926, as it would have increased its sales.

As Llona's remark suggests, the initial interest aroused by *Gatsby* had subsided by 1928, in the USA and UK as well as in France. The novel sometimes received brief mentions in the reviews of the three subsequent Fitzgerald books published in his lifetime, with the publication of *Tender is the Night*, in particular, stimulating comparisons with *Gatsby*. The 1934 reissue of *Gatsby* in a Modern Library edition with an introduction by Fitzgerald seemed to offer readers the chance to check out the respective merits of the two novels for themselves; but relatively few appear to have seized this opportunity. Fitzgerald's introduction is a fascinating piece of work, especially for its remarks on the *process* of writing *Gatsby*; but it was too unfocused and tangential to stimulate people to buy or read the book. He wanted to rewrite the introduction for a second impression, but sales were too low to justify its reprinting.

For the rest of the 1930s, *Gatsby* received little critical attention; the novel only started to get mentioned again when Fitzgerald died in December 1940. Several obituaries referred to it, but with varying judgements. For instance, *The New York Herald Tribune* called it 'compact and brilliant' and *The New Yorker* affirmed that it was 'one of the most scrupulously observed and beautifully written of American novels'; *The New York Times*, however, felt that while *Gatsby* 'caught superbly the spirit of a decade', it was 'not a book for the ages'. This view raised one of the most fundamental questions about *Gatsby* at this stage: would it last?

Two essays which appeared in the 1940s began to suggest that it might. William Troy's 'Scott Fitzgerald – The Authority of

Failure' (1945) saw Fitzgerald in *Gatsby* as using the technique of the 'intelligent but sympathetic observer' which he had derived from Conrad and James to split himself into two: the responsible Nick and the romantic Gatsby. Freed of a responsible self in this way, Gatsby can take off and become 'one of the few truly mythological creations in our recent literature'; endowed with a responsible self, Nick has to confront the painful experiences which arise through his friendship with Gatsby. Gatsby's story is finally one of failure; Nick's story is one of success as he transcends his pain and grows in moral perception. This positive view of Nick proved influential in the 1950s and still has its adherents today.

Like Troy, Arthur Mizener, in 'F. Scott Fitzgerald: The Poet of Borrowed Time' (1946), finds a split within *Gatsby*, but in his view the division is not primarily between the romantic Gatsby and the responsible Nick, but between East and West: the East represents urban sophistication and corruption; and the West, rural simplicity and virtue. Seen in this way, the novel becomes 'a kind of tragic pastoral' – pastoral being that literary form which celebrates an idealized version of rural life and, in European culture, goes back to the idylls of the ancient Greek poet Theocritus (*c.*300–*c.*260 BC), continues into the eighteenth century, and still has some residual life in the nineteenth and twentieth centuries. Thus Mizener places *Gatsby* in a distinguished lineage and provides an interpretation which will be the subject of future debate.

The most influential interpretation of the novel in the 1950s, however, would be that it was about 'the American Dream'. The first important expression of this view came in Lionel Trilling's *The Liberal Imagination* (1951), in an essay which claimed that 'Gatsby, divided between power and dream, comes inevitably to stand for America itself'. The idea that Gatsby stands for America is further developed in Edwin S. Fussell's essay 'Fitzgerald's Brave New World' (1952), where Gatsby is 'a very representative American' who is '[d]riven by forces that compel him towards the realization of romantic wonder' but is 'destroyed by the materials which the American experience offers as objects of passion'. But it was Marius Bewley's 'Scott Fitzgerald's criticism of America'

(1954) which offered the most developed 'American Dream' interpretation of the novel: 'Gatsby, the "mythic" embodiment of the
American dream, is shown to us in all his immature romanticism
. . . And yet the very grounding of [his] deficiencies is [his] good-
ness and faith in life, his compelling desire to realize all the possibilities of existence.' In 'The Waste Land of F. Scott Fitzgerald'
(1954), however, John W. Bicknell takes a much more demeaning
view of Gatsby and, by implication, of modern America; he sees
Gatsby's dreams as 'essentially infantile' and his death as pathetic,
not tragic: 'he is a victim, not a hero.'

The 'American Dream' interpretations of *Gatsby*, though powerful and persuasive in many ways, risked losing sight of the
energy of Fitzgerald's novel; in the attempt to establish its status
as serious literature, they were in danger of turning it into a
sombre and moralistic work. R. W. Stallman's '*Gatsby* and the
hole in time' (1955) challenged this perspective and is possibly
the liveliest and most observant essay on the novel to emerge in
the 1950s. Stallman accepts that *Gatsby* is about 'the American
dream' but argues that the novel is transformed into greatness by
its 'intricately patterned idea . . . of a myth-hero . . . a modern
Icarus . . . who . . . belongs not exclusively to one epoch of
American civilization but rather to all history inasmuch as all
history repeats in cycle form what Gatsby represents – America
itself'. In contrast to critics such as Troy who saw Nick as an
exemplar of moral growth, Stallman attacks him as 'a prig with
holier-than-thou airs'; against Mizener's view of the novel as 'a
tragic pastoral' which sets a good rural West against a corrupt
urban East, Stallman argues that this division, like all the others
in *Gatsby*, breaks down on closer attention: 'Nothing in the novel
is not confused . . . Everyone's identity overlaps another's.' As
well as being of great interest in its own right, Stallman's essay
anticipates later interpretations of *Gatsby* which focus on its contradictions and ambiguities.

In 1957 the first book-length critical study of Fitzgerald
appeared: *The Fictional Technique of F. Scott Fitzgerald* by James
E. Miller Jr., which, among much else, carefully analysed two of
the key narrative devices in *Gatsby* which we discussed in
Chapter 2: the modified first-person narrator and the rearrange-

ment of chronological order. Miller offers a helpful diagram of this rearrangement:

> Allowing X to stand for the straight chronological account of the summer of 1922, and A, B, C, D and E to represent the significant events of Gatsby's past, the nine chapters of *The Great Gatsby* may be charted: X, X, X, XCX, X, XBXCX, X, XCXDX, XEXAX (Miller (1964), p. 114).

This remains a helpful chart which can be checked against the text of the novel and used as a stimulus to consider the possible effects of the chronological rearrangement in relation both to specific sections and to the novel as a whole.

Miller's book completed the process, which had begun in the mid-1940s, of establishing *Gatsby*'s status as a work of considerable thematic and technical interest. This meant that critics in the 1960s could start to look more closely at specific aspects of it – as J. S. Westbrook did in 'Nature and Optics in *The Great Gatsby*' (1960–1). Westbrook affirms that the primary subject of the novel is 'the growth of an awareness' – Nick Carraway's – and that the narrative offers an account of Nick's initiation into the difficulties of seeing in a world which has become estranged from nature and offers only technological and commercial parodies of the natural. In this perspective it is Nick – rather than Gatsby – who becomes an image of America passing from youth into middle age and, more generally, an image of a phase of human life. Victor A. Doyno's 'Patterns in *The Great Gatsby*' (1966) focused on another aspect of the novel, the parallels and contrasts set up by its formal structure and rhetorical devices – for example, 'the repetition of dialogue, gesture, and detail', such as Gatsby's 'reaching' gesture which occurs at the end of Chapter 1 (p. 27) when he stretches out his arms towards the green light at the end of Daisy's dock, and in Chapter 8 (p. 159) when, leaving Louisville after his brief and lonely post-war return to the city, he stretches out his hand as if to grasp an airy memento of the place that Daisy irradiated.

Essays like those of Doyno and Westbrook demonstrated that *Gatsby* could sustain and reward close critical scrutiny but they tended to disconnect Fitzgerald's novel from the intense political and social debates of the 1960s. In the 1970s, however, as the fall-out from the 1960s began to be measured, attention began to turn again to the broader implications of *Gatsby* for questions of American national identity, and the 'American Dream' aspect of the novel started to be freshly explored, though in two contra-dictory directions, one of which led towards myth, the other towards history. Milton R. Stern's *The Golden Moment: The Novels of F. Scott Fitzgerald* (1970) affirms that Gatsby 'sums up our American desire to believe in a release from history', to believe in a redemption and realization that has already hap-pened at that founding moment evoked at the end of the novel. That moment is not primarily historical, however: it is 'sign and metaphor for human youth itself'. In this perspective, 'America is the golden moment in the history of the human race'; and Gatsby's life re-enacts 'that instant of history . . . in modern dress and in all its complex modifications'. Here Stern could be charged with perpetrating the kind of mystification in which, according to John F. Callahan's *The Illusions of a Nation: Myth and History in the Novels of F. Scott Fitzgerald* (1972), Nick Carraway is engaged in the famous concluding passage of *Gatsby*: putting 'a historical event in a metaphysical category.' Callahan argues that this may mean excluding uncomfortable aspects of history: 'Carraway forgets or does not regard as central the fact that this republic owed its life as much to its insti-tution of slavery and its colonial policy (really, a policy of exter-mination) toward the [Native Americans] as it did to the courage and democratic institutions of its citizens.'

The elimination of Native Americans from Nick's vision of the founding moment of the USA links up with the more general issue explored in Peter Gregg Slater's 'Ethnicity in *The Great Gatsby*' (1973). Ethnic questions had not been wholly absent from Fitzgerald criticism; the matter of Fitzgerald's representa-tion of Jews had been raised back in 1947 by Milton Hindus's 'F. Scott Fitzgerald and Literary Anti-Semitism', which argued that 'something important had been omitted' in all the praise for *Gatsby* – 'that viewed in a certain light the novel reads very much like an anti-Semitic document'. Discussion had been revived by

William Goldhurst's 'Literary Anti-Semitism in the 20's' (1962) and his *F. Scott Fitzgerald and his contemporaries* (1963) and continued through the 1960s, in, for example, Josephine Kopf's 'Meyer Wolfshiem and Robert Cohen: A study of Jewish type and stereotype' (1969). With regard to Fitzgerald's representation of African Americans, Keith Forrey's 'Negroes in the Fiction of F. Scott Fitzgerald' (1967) had charged that '[d]arker skinned individuals, when they do appear in Fitzgerald's fiction, are generally relegated to clownish and inferior roles' and that '[r]ich Negroes are almost by definition ludicrous' – to illustrate this latter point, he quotes Nick's description in Chapter 3 of *Gatsby* of the African Americans in the limousine. Slater, however, argues that *Gatsby* not only targets specific ethnic groups but also declares a much wider exclusion zone in its representation of Nick's 'ethnocentric interpretation of the American Dream' which casts out 'a whole section of the nation, the East, as well as those with intense ethnicity of a different sort than his own [Old American type]'.

As well as being ethnocentric, Nick's version of the American Dream, and perhaps Fitzgerald's, could be indicted with being androcentric, male-centred – it was '*man*' (my italics) who 'must have held his breath' at his first sight of the New World. While writing *Gatsby*, Fitzgerald himself had said that the novel had no important women characters and after its publication he suggested that its poor sales might be due to the aversion of female readers to its emotionally passive women figures. In the rapid development of feminism and feminist literary criticism in the 1970s, *Gatsby*'s representation of women came under closer scrutiny. For example, in ' "Only her hairdresser . . .": another look at Daisy Buchanan', Joan S. Korenman homed in on what might seem a relatively small matter – the inconsistency in the text of *Gatsby* whereby Daisy's hair sometimes seems to be blonde and sometimes dark. Korenman suggests that the inconsistency partly 'reflects a fundamental duality in Daisy herself, her simultaneous embodiment of traits associated with the fair and the dark women of romantic literature . . . [she] is both cool innocent princess and sensuous *femme fatale*'. Korenman is primarily concerned with Daisy as a cultural signifier, but Leland

Person, Jr., in ' "Herstory" and Daisy Buchanan' (1978) uses the text to try to see Daisy as a human being with 'her own complex story, her own desires and needs'. Daisy, Person suggests, is 'more victim than victimizer' and she is 'victimized by a male tendency to project a self-satisfying, yet ultimately dehumanizing, image on woman'. In *Fitzgerald's new women: harbingers of change* (1988), Sarah Beebe Fryer similarly contends that Daisy is 'a victim of a complex network of needs and desires' who 'deserves more pity than blame' and whose 'confusion over her relationships with the two principal men in her life' is not simply a personal weakness but 'reflects the gender confusion that was rampant during Fitzgerald's era'.

That gender confusion may also relate to Nick's sexuality. The sense that there were homoerotic subtexts in *Gatsby* goes back at least to Lionel Trilling, who in his *Liberal Imagination* essay had called Jordan Baker 'vaguely homosexual'. Seventeen years later, the issue resurfaced, not in academic literary criticism, but in the novel *Getting Straight* (1967) by Ken Kolb (born 1926) and in the 1970 film based on the book. But the essay that put the matter on the critical map was the disarmingly entitled 'Another reading of *The Great Gatsby*' (1979) by Keath Fraser. With close attention to textual detail and implication, Fraser suggests that there are homoerotic undertones in the scene between Nick and Chester McKee, Nick's fascination with Tom's masculine body and the contrasts the novel establishes between Tom and Gatsby, and Tom and Wilson. Fraser argues for an acknowledgement of 'the full play of sexuality' in this erotically anarchic novel of 'potency and impotency, of jealous sex and Platonic love'.

In *Gatsby* studies, Fraser's essay was the climax of a pioneering decade, the 1970s, which had broached the previously taboo topics of the novel's ethnic, gender and sexual representations and exclusions. In the 1980s and 1990s, there were, among much interesting work, four studies which, from the vantage point of the early twenty-first century, especially stand out for their originality, continued relevance, and scope for further development. The landmark critique of the 1980s was Richard Godden's '*The Great Gatsby*: Glamour on the Turn' (1982) which sees Gatsby as functioning like a Brechtian actor to break the audience's comforting illusions and recall it to material reality – most notably when he says that Daisy's voice is 'full of money'. For Gatsby, 'Daisy's glamour is glamour on the turn, and he would have Nick know it, but Nick will not be distracted from his simple identifications with "love" . . . Gatsby loves Daisy because she is his point of access to a dominant class. Marriage would allow him to harden his liquid assets'. Valuable though Godden's demystifying approach is, however, it did not anticipate the way in which, as the 1980s proceeded, money would shake off its shame, assume its own glamour, and cast the alibi of love aside.

The glamour of money in the 1980s would be bound up, in complex ways, with the development of postmodernist theory, but although *Gatsby* could be seen to anticipate key elements of postmodernism, there have been surprisingly few postmodernist readings of the novel. A scintillating exception can, however, be found in Patty White's *Gatsby's Party: The System and the List in Contemporary Narrative* (1992). White sees Gatsby, created from a concept and inhabiting the hyperspace of West Egg, as an example of what the postmodernist thinker Jean Baudrillard (born 1929) calls a 'simulacrum', a copy with no original; Nick, like an anthropologist, 'approaches Gatsby as if he were an alien culture, codifying his relationships, recording the reports of informants, tracing and translating his creation myths'. The image of an anthropologist approaching an alien culture could also apply to Ronald Berman's approach to Gatsby – and to *Gatsby*. As he points out in '*The Great Gatsby* and the twenties' (2002), the novel 'was written before most of its readers were born' and 'inhabits a different world'. It is that world which Berman seeks to retrieve and reconstruct in two fascinating books: *The Great Gatsby and Modern Times* (1994), which sets the novel in the context of the popular culture of the period, and *The Great Gatsby and Fitzgerald's World of Ideas* (1997), which sets the novel in the context of contemporary philosophical and intellectual debates. Berman's work effectively invalidates the opposition employed by the *New York Times* 1940 obituary of Fitzgerald when it claimed that *Gatsby* 'caught superbly the spirit of a decade' but was 'not a book for the ages'. It is rather that *Gatsby* captures superbly the spirit of a decade and, partly because of that, is *also* a book for the ages: its durability is demonstrated by its capacity to go on generating the kind of criticism we have considered in this section and by the sales it now enjoys. As the next section will show, however, its commercial success was not always so assured.

PUBLISHING HISTORY

Gatsby was published by Scribner's in New York on 10 April 1925 with a print run of 20,870. The book cost $2.00 and had a superb dust jacket by Francis Cugat which showed a woman's vast eyes and lips suspended in a darkening blue sky above a brightly lit amusement park which is tiny by comparison. The blurb suggested both the richness of the novel and the difficulty of definition it presented, calling it glamorous, ironical, compassionate, lyrical, brutal, magical and living. This difficulty of defining *Gatsby* may have contributed to what Maxwell Perkins, in a wire to Fitzgerald of 20 April 1925, called its 'doubtful' commercial fate; the sales crept up comparatively slowly, from 12,000 in early May to 16,000 in early July, but they had still not quite reached 20,000 by October. Fitzgerald was entitled to a 15 per cent royalty on each copy sold, and the first printing earned enough – $6,261 – to cancel his debt of $6,000 to Scribner's, but with only $261 left over. There was a second printing of 3,000 copies in August 1925; but some of these were still unsold on Fitzgerald's death in 1940. A total printing of 23,870 was less than half of the 49,075 copies of *This Side of Paradise* which had been printed by the end of 1921, or the 50,000 copies of *The Beautiful and Damned* run off in 1922.

William Collins, the British publishers of Fitzgerald's two earlier novels, had a first-refusal option on *Gatsby* but turned it down because they felt the book would be too alien for an English audience. Chatto and Windus brought it out in 1926 in a print run of 1,616 copies. The book cost 7s 6d (37.5p) and sold 1,100 copies in 1926; in 1927, the price was reduced to 2s 6d (12.5p) or 2s (10p) and 350 more copies found purchasers. According to these figures, there should have been 166 copies remaining from the original print run; some of these would have been review copies, but it is unclear what happened to all of them. The total royalties amounted to £32.15s.2d (£32.76). The British fiction magazine *Argosy* published a complete version of *Gatsby* in its August 1937 issue, but another edition in book form did not appear in the UK until 1948.

The first French translation of the novel, *Gatsby le magnifique*, also came out in 1926 in the 'Collection européene' of the Paris publishing house of Kra, at a price of 13 francs 50, or 20 francs for an edition on vellum paper. Fitzgerald himself thought the translation, by Victor Llona, sounded 'wonderful', but his knowledge of French was poor, and André le Vot, a very perceptive Fitzgerald critic and biographer, has pointed out many errors in Llona's rendition. His translation continued to be used, however, in subsequent French editions from Sagittaire in 1946, Le Club Français du Livre in 1952 and 1959, Grasset in 1959 and Livre de Poche in 1962. A new French translation by Jacques Tournier appeared in 1976.

The French translation was followed by translations into Norwegian in 1927 and into German in 1932. In the USA, a Modern Library edition of *Gatsby* came out in 1934, the year in which *Tender is the Night* was published; it was priced at 95 cents and had an introduction by Fitzgerald. Any hope that this might revive the commercial and critical fortunes of the book did not last long, however: it sold poorly and was soon struck off the Modern Library list. A new edition did not appear again until after Fitzgerald's death, when Scribner's brought out a volume edited by Edmund Wilson which contained his version of *The Last Tycoon* (Wilson's title for the unfinished novel on which Fitzgerald had been working when he died), *Gatsby*, and five short stories, one of which belongs to the Gatsby group – 'Absolution'. Precise figures do not seem to be available for the first print run of Wilson's volume, but 3,000 copies has been proposed as a probable total. The volume came out on 27 October 1941 at a price of $2.75. It was reprinted before the end of the year and then again in 1945, 1947 and 1948; the sixth printing, in 1951, left out the short stories, but retained *Gatsby*. Meanwhile, in 1942, Scribner's had brought out a small reprint of *Gatsby* in an individual volume.

The year of 1945 was a bumper one for editions of *Gatsby*. As well as appearing in a volume with *The Last Tycoon* and the five short stories, it featured, along with *Tender* and nine short stories, in two impressions of a Viking *Portable Fitzgerald* edited by the well-known writer and critic Dorothy Parker (1893–1967). It also came out singly as a Bantam paperback costing 25 cents and in an Armed Services edition of 155,000 copies that were given away to military personnel for free. The following year, the volume *Great American Short Novels* included *Gatsby*; New Directions brought out *Gatsby* in the New Classic series with an introduction by Lionel Trilling, and the Bantam paperback went through two reprints. In 1949, a third and fourth impression of the *Portable Fitzgerald* appeared and Grosset and Duncan published an edition of the novel that would tie in with the Alan Ladd movie version released in that year.

The later 1940s also saw further translations of the novel, into Swedish (1946), Dutch and Danish (1948) and Italian (1950); these suggested that the novel was developing a significant international presence outside the USA and UK. In the UK, Grey Walls Press brought out a small hardback edition which had reasonable sales and went through two printings. Penguin published the first paperback edition in 1950 and it remains in print today. The first volume of the Bodley Head hardback edition of Fitzgerald came out in 1958 and consisted of *Gatsby* and *The Last Tycoon*, with an introduction by the well-known if then rather unfashionable novelist and playwright J. B. Priestley (1894–1984). Cambridge University Press brought out *Gatsby* as the first volume of its Fitzgerald critical edition in 1991 and the galley proof version of the novel, under the title of *Trimalchio*, in 2000.

In the USA itself, the sales of *Gatsby* continued to grow as the twentieth century advanced, stimulated by the increasingly widespread inclusion of the novel on academic courses, by film and TV adaptations, by the expanding volume of critical commentary, and by the continuing popular interest in the lives of Scott and Zelda. Scribner's sales of a book which had lain unsold in their warehouse at the time of Fitzgerald's death reached 12,000 in 1957, 36,000 in 1958 and over 100,000 annually by 1960. By the end of the 1960s, annual sales were around 300,000 a year and they have stayed at this level. Fitzgerald once remarked, contrasting himself with Ernest Hemingway, that he spoke with the authority of failure; commercially as well as critically, *Gatsby* now speaks with the authority of success.

STUDY QUESTIONS FOR CHAPTER 4

1. This chapter has explored a range of interpretations of *Gatsby* – for example, as a book about the American Dream, about the growth of an awareness, about American history and society, about gender, and about money. Which of these interpretations do you find most convincing, and why?
2. *Gatsby* is much more accessible than a Modernist text such as James Joyce's *Ulysses*, but critical appreciation of Fitzgerald's novel nonetheless took a long time to develop, not really getting under way until the 1950s. What do you think were the reasons for this delay?
3. Why do you think the sales of *Gatsby* took off after the Second World War and why does the novel continue to sell well today? How would you market it to ensure continued sales in the twenty-first century?

CHAPTER 5

ADAPTATION, INTERPRETATION AND INFLUENCE

Gatsby was quick to move onto stage and screen, with both a theatre production and a silent film in 1926, the year after the book's publication. There appears to be no published script of the play, and the print of the silent film seems to have been lost, but it is possible, from surviving documentation, to gain some idea of what they were like. There have been two more film adaptations: a black-and-white version starring Alan Ladd in 1949, and a colour version starring Robert Redford in 1974. On US TV, there was a one-hour NBC adaptation with Robert Montgomery as Gatsby in the series *Robert Montgomery Presents* on 9 May 1955 and a 90-minute CBS production with Robert Ryan as Gatsby in the *Playhouse 90* series on 26 June 1958. British TV showed a 90-minute version with Toby Stephens as Gatsby on BBC1 on 29 March 2000. Little information about the US TV versions appears to be available; we shall focus on each of the other adaptations in date order, and then move on to consider the *Gatsby* opera which premiered late in 1999.

THE PLAY (1926)

The script of the stage version of *Gatsby* was written by Owen Davis (1874–1956), a dramatist whose play *Icebound* (1923), a drama about a repressive, 'icebound' family, had won the Pulitzer Prize for drama three years earlier. In his adaptation, Davis makes several significant changes. The most striking is his rearrangement of the chronological structure by inserting a prologue set in the Fays' sitting room in Louisville in 1917 and introducing three new characters. Mrs Fay, Daisy's mother, is concerned about the young lieutenant with whom her daughter has sneaked out, and she talks about him first with Sally, her African-American maid, and then with Major Carson, who is able to provide her with a complete biography of Gatsby, supplied by army intelligence, from his boyhood up to Dan Cody's death. Mrs Fay whets the audience's appetite for Gatsby by calling him absurd, dangerous, romantic as a gipsy, handsome, arrogant, ambitious and over-weeningly proud; after she and Major Carson go out, Gatsby and Daisy come in. Gatsby talks about his love for her and his boyhood dreams, and takes a rhapsodic leave; Tom Buchanan then enters – in the play he, like Gatsby, is in the army, and he has come from New York especially to see Daisy before he departs for France – and Daisy receives him flirtatiously.

In this prologue, as in other parts of the play, Davis turns segments of Nick's narrative of Gatsby's life into direct statements by Gatsby. He also updates the play from 1922 to 1925; displaces Nick into little more than a plot device for reuniting Gatsby and Daisy; replaces Nick's nameless Finn with an English-speaking and more loquacious Mrs Morton whose conversations with Nick help with the exposition of the action; fuses Gatsby's parties into one and pushes them mostly offstage, setting Act 1 in Nick's bungalow and Acts 2 and 3 in Gatsby's library; turns Gatsby into a man who, as the play proceeds, faces financial ruin and imminent arrest; cuts out the valley of ashes and the billboard; and makes Wilson not a mechanic but a chauffeur who works first for Tom and then for Gatsby and who, in the end, shoots both Gatsby and Myrtle. These changes seemed to add up to an effective play, however.

The director of the Broadway production was George Cukor (1899–1983), who would later turn from the stage to the screen and direct a range of well-received films, including some notable movie adaptations of novels and plays – for instance, *Little Women* (1933), *David Copperfield* (1934), *The Philadelphia Story* (1940, based on Philip Barry's 1939 play of the same title) and *My Fair Lady* (1964, based on George Bernard Shaw's *Pygmalion*, 1916). Cukor knew Fitzgerald's fiction and liked

Davis's script; only minor changes were made in production. Gatsby was played by James Rennie (1890–1965), a handsome Canadian with a good voice, and Daisy by the distinguished actress Florence Eldridge (1901–88). Jordan Baker was played by Catherine Willard (*c*.1900–54), whose performance Cukor recalled as 'marvellous': stylish, 'rather deadpan' and 'cool'; Eliot Cabot, a scion of the elite Boston family who was, according to Cukor, 'very good looking, slightly brutal looking', took on the role of Tom Buchanan; and Charles Dickson (*c*.1860–1927), a former comedy star, was Wolfshiem – Cukor recalled him as a very subtle performer who seemed to *be* rather than *act* the part.

The stage version of *Gatsby* opened at the Ambassador Theatre on Broadway on Tuesday 2 February 1926, less than nine months after the publication of the novel. Fitzgerald and Zelda were in France and never saw the production but Fitzgerald's agent, Harold Ober, sent him a telegram on 4 February saying that the audience were 'enthusiastic' about an adaptation which 'carried [the] glamour of the story'. The critics also enthused; an unidentified clipping in Fitzgerald's scrapbook has a round-up of favourable review comments on the play: J. Brooks Atkinson of *The New York Times* felt, like Ober, that the 'dramatic version retains most of the novel's peculiar glamour'; Alexander Woollcott in *The New York World* asserted that the 'fine, vivid novel . . . is carried over on to the stage with almost the minimum of spilling', and Percy Hammond in *The New York Herald Tribune* praised Davis's 'deft shifting of the book's essential episodes' as 'a marvel of rearrangement and dovetailing', found that the 'speech of characters is retained in much of its clear-cut veracity' and affirmed that the dramatization was 'so able that it managed to emphasize the subtle qualities of Mr. Fitzgerald's study of a golden vagabond'.

The play ran for 112 performances and closed only when James Rennie had to go to England to be with his wife who was attending on her ailing mother. When he returned to the USA, he took up the role of Gatsby again and the production, with some changes in other cast members, went on a successful tour that included performances in Chicago from 1 August to 2 October. Fitzgerald wrote to Ober that as the play had been 'something of a *sucès d'estime* [a success in terms of critical appreciation] and put in my pocket seventeen or eighteen thousand . . . I should be, and am, well contented'. The film would earn him much more: he sold the rights for $45,000.

THE FIRST FILM (1926)

The silent film version of *The Great Gatsby* was produced by Famous Players-Lasky-Paramount Pictures and directed by Herbert Brenon (1880–1958), who had a high reputation in the 1920s and who had just completed his still-remembered movie version of *Beau Geste* (1926, based on the best-selling romantic adventure story of the same title published in 1924, by P. C. Wren (1885–1941)). Interestingly, two women had a hand in writing the movie: the treatment was by Elizabeth Meehan (1894–1967) and the screenplay was by Becky Gardiner (1806–?). The film apparently stayed fairly close to the plot of the play, though with some variations; for example, one shot in Meehan's treatment was a flashback to Daisy in Louisville as a young married woman and mother holding her child tightly and feeling apprehensive about Gatsby's return. Although Gatsby reawakens her love when he comes back, she turns against him in the Plaza Hotel scene after Tom has exposed him as a bootlegger – the implication seems to be that she rejects him because he is a criminal rather than because, as in the novel, he makes the impossible demand that she should say she never loved Tom. After Myrtle's death, Daisy wants to confess that she killed her, but does not do so; when Nick phones to tell her and Tom of Gatsby's murder, there is no reply and the Buchanans leave New York unaware of it. They become reconciled and the film ends with an affirmation of family values: the final shot shows, in the words of one reviewer, 'Daisy and her husband Tom and their tot draped beautifully on the porch of their happy home'.

The part of Gatsby was played by Warner Baxter (1891–1951), a popular figure in silent melodramas who would later successfully move into talking pictures and become best known for his role as the theatre director in *42nd Street* (1933). Lois Wilson (1895–1988), previously typecast, according to one reviewer of the film, as 'the demure heroine of some scores of placid screen romances', took on the very different role of Daisy. Neil Hamilton (1899–1984) played Nick Carraway, Hale Hamilton (1883–1942) was Tom Buchanan, Carmelita Geraghty (1901–66) played Jordan Baker, Georgia Hale (1903–85) tackled Myrtle, and Wilson was played by William Powell (1892–1984), who would later become best known as Nick Charles, the private eye in the *Thin Man* film series (1934–47), the first of which was adapted from the novel of the same title published in 1932 by Dashiell Hammett (1894–1961). George Nash (1873–1944) played Charles Wolf, the film's version of Wolfshiem, and there were two extra characters, whose functions remain obscure – 'Lord Digby', played by Eric Blore (1887–1959) and 'Bert', played by 'Gunboat' Smith (1887–1974).

The eight-reel, 80-minute, 7,296-foot-long silent film of *Gatsby* opened at the Rivoli Theatre in New York in 1926. The review clippings pasted in Fitzgerald's scrapbook, none of which indicates a source, reveal a mixed response. 'Mae Tinée' gave it a rave: 'a picture that grips every step of the way . . . Its people are real and their actions and reactions wholly comprehensible . . . The entire cast . . . is irreproachable.' An anonymous review called it 'mighty good' and said that the 'picturization' had 'changed the novel a bit but; not enough to hurt' and had left 'plenty of the Fitzgerald touch'; it generally praised the cast but found Lois Wilson much better than Warner Baxter. Eileen Creelman, however, applauded the 'understanding and courage' of Baxter's performance and particularly referred to the scene in which Gatsby displays his shirts; but she did acknowledge that Lois Wilson stole the show and caused 'a sensation' in the audience, especially in a scene 'with a bobbed-haired Lois quite hopelessly drunk in a bathtub' – presumably the film's version of the scene in Chapter 4 of the novel, in Jordan Baker's narrative, when the drunken Daisy is put in a cold bath (pp. 82–3). Creelman did criticize some aspects of the film, however; for example, she felt that it sometimes followed the novel almost too closely and that the intertitles could seem 'unnecessary and annoying'. The complaint about the titles was echoed more eloquently by John S. Cohen Jr, who found these 'wordy interruptions', with their 'generally bad English, inappropriate wording, length, and cheap fictional rubber stamping', stopped the visual flow, making the film 'about as smooth pictorially as sandpaper'. He did concede, however, that *Gatsby* had one claim to uniqueness: it 'boasts of the longest bit of reading matter in the history of the cinema' with an inter-title that 'stretches from the top of the screen to the bottom'.

Cohen's negative response seems to have been shared by the cinema public, if not necessarily for the same reasons. The film lasted only two weeks at the Rivoli Theatre and had no success elsewhere. It did, however, have one significant admirer: the nov-elist and short-story writer John O'Hara (1905–70), who knew and deeply appreciated Fitzgerald's fiction. O'Hara later recalled his 'exultation at the end of the picture when I saw that Paramount had done an honest job, true to the book, true to what Fitzgerald had intended'. After talking pictures arrived, O'Hara hoped to script a sound remake of the silent film; the actor Clark Gable (1901–60) had discussed the possibility of another film of *Gatsby* with Fitzgerald himself and encouraged O'Hara in his attempt to buy the screen rights of the novel. But nothing came of this; 23 years elapsed between the silent *Gatsby* and the first sound version, and by then Fitzgerald was dead.

THE SECOND FILM (1949)

The second film of *The Great Gatsby* is probably best known as 'the Alan Ladd version', after its leading man. Ladd (1913–64) was especially famous at this time for his 'tough guy' roles – or, more precisely, with roles that combined toughness of words and actions with a physical delicacy and frailty that suggested vulner-ability. He had established his image by acting with Veronica Lake (1919–73) in two films of 1942 – *This Gun for Hire* (based on the novel *This Gun for Sale* (1936), by Graham Greene (1904–91)) and *The Glass Key* (1942) – and consolidated it in *The Blue Dahlia* (1946), where he portrayed a heroic ex-bomber pilot suspected of killing his wife. In *Gatsby*, however, he was paired with the char-acter actress Betty Field (1918–73). Among other members of the cast were Barry Sullivan (1912–94) as Tom; Macdonald Carey (1913–94) as Nick; Ruth Hussey (1911–2005) as Jordan; Shelley

Winters (1920–2006) as Myrtle; Howard da Silva (1909–86) as Wilson; Elisha Cook Jr. (1903–95) as Klipspringer; Ed Begley (1901–70) as Myron Lupus (this film's version of Wolfshiem); Henry Hull (1890–1977) as Dan Cody, Carole Mathews (born 1920) as Ella Cody, Nicholas Joy (1894–1964) as the Owl Man and Tito Vuolo (1893–1962) as Mavromichaelis.

As this cast list suggests, the 1949 film tried to get in more of the novel than the Owen Davis stage play or the 1926 silent movie: Dan Cody, Ella, Michaelis and Klipspringer are all included. The writers were the British screenwriter and novelist Cyril Hume (1900–66) and the American screenwriter who would later script ten James Bond movies, Richard Maibaum (1909–91), and in some ways they do stay closer to the novel, especially in their use of flashbacks to tell the backstory of Gatsby's life – this is where Dan Cody comes in – and in their deployment of the eyes of Dr T. J. Eckleburg at the start and end of the film. But there were also considerable changes. As Fitzgerald's novel, in Maibaum's words, 'dealt with unpunished adultery, unpunished manslaughter, and an unpunished moral accessory to a murder', it was necessary, in order to comply with the Hollywood production code, to make the film more moralistic, so that even the apparently less moral or amoral characters – Jordan Baker, Gatsby himself – show contrition. Most strikingly, in a motif familiar from 1930s gangster movies such as *Angels with Dirty Faces* (1938), the importance of not setting a bad example to boys who might be impressed by the glamour of gangsterism is stressed when Gatsby, without realizing Wilson is about to kill him, decides to turn himself in to the police and says to Nick: 'What's going to happen to kids like Jimmy Gatz if guys like me don't tell them we're wrong?' In a paradox also familiar from those 1930s movies, however, the importance of setting a good example is contradicted by the visual excitement of the gangster in action, an excitement which the film stresses with added scenes that are not from the novel, such as the opening montage of hijackings and shoot-outs in which Gatsby is seen to play a key role. The closeness of the film to the movies of the previous decade is emphasized not only by generic features but also by the updating of the action from 1922 to 1928.

The director of the film was Elliott Nugent (1896–1980), a stage actor, producer and dramatist whose excursions into direction were relatively infrequent and who had been most successful directing comic movies, particularly the comedy thriller *The Cat and the Canary* (1939), starring Bob Hope (1903–2003). Nugent thought *Gatsby* 'Fitzgerald's best novel and perhaps the best of all American novels' and the prospect of shooting it made him so anxious that, the day before filming was scheduled to start, he went to the tenth-floor fire escape of the Roosevelt Hotel on Hollywood Boulevard with the intention of leaping off. The moment passed, however, and he went ahead with the film and finished it. Perhaps his close encounter with mortal despair fed fruitfully into the picture, which has been regarded as his best.

Nugent felt that his *Gatsby* got good reviews and this is borne out to some extent by the critical response. For example, Jesse Zunser in *Cue* (16 July 1949) felt that the picture caught much of the atmosphere of the 1920s, even if it failed to develop its central characters, espeaially Gatsby. On the other hand, Bosley Crowther in *The New York Times* (14 July 1949) charged that it 'barely reflected' the Prohibition epoch and suggested that Paramount's primary motive for making the film was to provide 'a standard conveyance for the image of its charm boy, Alan Ladd' – a comment that does not quite take into account the fact that Gatsby himself could be seen, in part, as a 'charm boy' and that in that respect Ladd might be seen as the right choice for the role. In the *New Yorker* (23 July 1949), John McCarten also went for Ladd, claiming that his acting was as stiff as that of a pallbearer, and deprecating the 'jittery carryings-on' of Betty Field's Daisy – although again it might be said that in the novel stiffness is one of Gatsby's characteristics and jitteriness is one of Daisy's. Clearly, however, reviewers were not overwhelmed by the film and there was scope for another one. This would not, however, appear for another quarter of a century.

THE THIRD FILM (1974)

If the second *Gatsby* film had been seen as a vehicle for its male lead, *The Great Gatsby* film of 1974 could be seen as a vehicle for both its leading co-stars, Robert Redford (born 1937) and Mia Farrow (born 1945), both of whom were already famous when the film was made. The casting of each of them, however, raised doubts in some quarters. One of the shrewdest remarks on Redford came from Howard da Silva, who had played Wilson in the 1949 *Gatsby* and who, in an interesting piece of casting, was given the role of Wolfshiem in this one; da Silva greatly admired Redford's acting abilities but felt that 'he could never play a man from the opposite side of the tracks'. In contrast, Ladd, who, in actual life, really *was* from the other side of the tracks, 'could and did'. A crucial criticism of Mia Farrow's Daisy came from Fitzgerald's daughter, Scottie, who thought Farrow a 'fine actress' but felt she had been unable to convey the 'intensely Southern' nature of Daisy's character.

The director was Jack Clayton (1921–95), whose best-known previous credit was *Room at the Top* (1958), a taut, effective adaptation of the 1957 novel of the same title by John Braine (1922–86) about a poor boy who eventually gets the rich girl only to realize that he really wants another woman. In a curious collaboration, however, the film was scripted by a figure who was already a bigger directorial name than Clayton: Francis Ford Coppola (born 1939), whose second *Godfather* film came out in the same year as *The Great Gatsby*. There was some explicit disagreement over which scenes to include – for instance, Clayton put in the scene at Gatsby's funeral while Coppola had wanted the film to end at the point where Gatsby's father, in his son's mansion for the first time, sees the photograph of Daisy and says 'Who's the girl?' The final film was a long one – about 2 hours and 20 minutes – and would have been even longer but for some cuts, one of which was certainly unfortunate in that it removed a key motif of the book: the scenes with an owl-eyed man, played by Tom Ewell (1905–94), were seen by some early cinema audiences but then removed, and they do not appear to have been made available yet on DVD.

The 1974 film has a much more straightforward chronological structure than either the novel or the 1949 movie; there is only one extended flashback to Gatsby and Daisy's Louisville romance, and that is visually vague. Sometimes scenes in the novel are altered to questionable effect: for example, the film eliminates Nick's gaffe on his first visit to a Gatsby party when he starts talking to a fellow First World War veteran about Gatsby without realizing that the veteran *is* Gatsby – an error that gives Gatsby the opportunity, once he has corrected Nick's mistake, to confer his smile on him for the first time. In the 1974 film, a minder draws Nick out of the garden and takes him up in a lift to Gatsby's office, where Redford provides a smile that does not seem to spring naturally out of the situation and looks like a low budget toothpaste ad – an ironic impression given that the film was the most expensive *Gatsby* to date, costing around $6.5 million, a large sum for a movie at the time.

The film had a poor critical reception. For instance, *The New York Times* (31 March 1974) declared 'They've turned *Gatsby* to Goo', while Stanley Kauffmann in the *New Republic* (13 April 1974) found it a 'long, slow, sickening bore'. Penelope Gilliat in *The New Yorker* (1974) was less dismissive, calling it a 'stately' film with 'much kindness and beauty' but she also felt it was 'mistakenly long', with too many repeated or extended shots and superfluous voice-over commentary which reiterated points that had already been made visually. As well as complaints of sentimentality and tedium, there was also a sense that the film failed to engage with the novel's critique of the American Dream – a critique that could have seemed particularly relevant in the aftermath of the Vietnam War and Watergate. Although the film was commercially successful, it seemed to lose too much of the book to be critically satisfying. Another quarter of a century would elapse, however, before a further *Gatsby* film appeared, and this time it would have an English actor in the lead role.

THE TV FILM (2000)

The 2000 made-for-TV film was jointly produced by Granada Entertainment in the UK and A and E Cable Network in the US, and brought together the English actor Toby Stephens (born 1969) and the American actress Mira Sorvino (born 1967) in the lead roles of Gatsby and Daisy. Paul Rudd (born 1969) played

Nick Carraway and Martin Donovan (born 1957) was Tom Buchanan. The screenplay was by John McLaughlin. Elements eliminated from the 1974 film are restored here: for example, the owl-eyed man appears in the library, where he explicitly draws attention to his resemblance to Dr. T. J. Eckleburg, recurs in a later party scene, and appears at Gatsby's funeral to deliver the 'son-of-a-bitch' epitaph.

There are also new departures, however. As if to stress that this narrative will play with time, the beginning of the film provides an almost immediate flash-forward to Gatsby's death; we see Nick and hear his voice-over delivering a very much shortened and edited version of the novel's opening paragraphs and we then see Gatsby floating on his mattress in his swimming pool and being shot. The image of the body in, or, in this case, on the swimming pool recalls the opening of *Sunset Boulevard* (1950), directed by Billy Wilder (1906–2002). In contrast to the graphic violence of the shooting scene in the 1974 *The Great Gatsby*, where several bullets puncture Gatsby's mattress and he sinks into a swirl of his own blood, the 2000 film is more faithful to the novel's image of the laden mattress staying on the surface. It does, however, add an extra detail, showing Gatsby's hand opening and letting a pair of cuff buttons fall into the water and sink to the bottom of the pool. This is a curious transposition of the motif of cuff buttons which, in the novel, sets up a sinister link between Wolfshiem's 'finest specimens of human molars' (p. 78) and the cuff buttons that Nick thinks Tom may be going to buy when he meets him in Fifth Avenue near the end of the novel (p. 186); here, it is Daisy who gives Gatsby the cuff buttons during their Louisville romance and his relinquishment of them in death symbolizes the end of his dream. It could be said, however, that the sinister associations remain; it is, after all, Gatsby's love for Daisy which will prove lethal to him. Made on a relatively low budget, and much less widely hyped than the 1974 film, the 2000 version stays closer to the novel and the changes that it does make seem intelligible and interesting rather than arbitrary, as they often do in the Redford/Farrow version.

THE OPERA (2000)

On 20 December 1999, 11 days before the start of the new millennium, the world premiere of the opera of *The Great Gatsby* by John Harbison (born 1938) was held at the Metropolitan Opera House in New York. The Met had commissioned the opera to commemorate the 25th anniversary of the debut of the conductor James Levine. Harbison had long been interested in writing an opera based on *Gatsby* but had found it difficult to obtain the rights to do so; he was able to go ahead, however, once the novel came out of copyright and entered the public domain. Harbison knew the text of *Gatsby* well and wrote not only the music, but also his own libretto, apart from the 1920s-style pop song lyrics which were provided by Murray Horwitz (born 1949). In writing the libretto, Harbison recalled, he 'found most of what I required somewhere in Fitzgerald's novel, coming to the surface when I needed it'.

Harbison's score for the opera draws on traditional classical music, employing harmony, polyphony and counterpoint, and on 1920s popular music – foxtrots, two-steps, tangos, rumbas and torch songs. This corresponds to his sense that 'the characters in *Gatsby* live in a world of the sounds of their time – radio music, dance bands, car horns, fog horns on Long Island sound, the beat of the popular music of the mid-20s'. The opera was well received by reviewers, who sometimes praised it in terms that resemble the ways in which literary critics had praised the novel (no dates are available for these reviews as they were taken from a website – see Chapter 6 for details). For example, Richard Dyer in *The Boston Globe* echoed those critics who had commended the intricate patterning of Fitzgerald's *Gatsby* when he affirmed that Harbison's score had not only 'immediate appeal' but also 'a network of internal reference so intricate it will take years of repeated hearings to understand'. Similarly, Peter G. Davis in the *New York Magazine* called Harbison's adaptation 'a cunningly organized structure of dramatic parallels and musical interconnections'. In contrast, Mark Swed, in the *Los Angeles Times*, suggested that the opera had, in a sense, simplified Fitzgerald's novel, but in a way that retained rather than removed its crucial dynamic elements and brought out the operatic quality that was in the novel already: he felt that Harbison 'has succeeded in creating a straightforward dramatic narrative, with all the properly operatic elements of languid love, hot sex, jealousy, murder, party scenes and a funeral'. For Swed, however, the opera's greatest achievement was to dramatize 'the subversive nature of the novel, eroding the forced roaring '20s gaiety and emptiness with dark currents'. Reviewers singled out various parts of the opera for praise: Davis homed in on 'Carraway's rhapsodic eulogy over Gatsby's coffin', calling it 'a gorgeous piece of vocal writing'; Dyer found Gatsby and Daisy's love duet 'glorious'; Joshua Kosman in the *San Francisco Chronicle* found a 'heart-wrenching . . . power' in the 'tender lyricism of . . . Daisy's first soliloquy, Gatsby's final reverie recalling the magic of their first love, and even Nick's oddly minimalist evocation of a winter train ride through Wisconsin'; and Heidi Waleson in *The Wall Street Journal* called the 'languid duets' between Daisy and Jordan 'masterpieces of vocal loveliness and character painting' and described how, in the premiere, the 'astonishing mezzo Lorraine Hunt Lieberson filled the Met with Myrtle's earthy desires. Her two arias, one in each act, were the hottest moments in the show. Her rhythmic taunting cry of "Daisy! Daisy!", which makes Tom slug her and break her nose, is electric'.

It seems that the opera of *Gatsby*, written and composed by a figure who has a deep understanding and knowledge of Fitzgerald's novel and who combines literary and musical talent, could be the most complete creative adaptation of that novel into another medium which we have so far seen. Peter Davis felt the opera has 'definite survival potential' and if it does endure it could take its place alongside Fitzgerald's *Gatsby* as Verdi's operas have taken their place alongside the Shakespeare plays which they complement and sometimes even surpass. In the meantime – that telling phrase from 'Ain't we got fun' – the opera demonstrates *Gatsby*'s continuing power to inform, shape and inspire American culture.

THE LITERARY INFLUENCE

As a novel, *Gatsby* is a hard, perhaps impossible act to follow. Few people who have tried their hand at creative writing will fail to recognize that, when it comes to fictional prose, Fitzgerald can cut it – that his style has a grace, a power, a delicate strength, a resourcefulness of rhythm, image and diction that reaches its highest pitch of achievement in *Gatsby* and that is intimidating for would-be imitators. Hemingway developed a prose technique that seemed transferable and he has had many self-elected disciples, those who have tried to go and do likewise. Fitzgerald teaches a different lesson: that each writer should develop their own, unique style to the fullest. If this lesson is true, the most fitting response to *Gatsby* would be to strike out for something quite different; and American writers have done this. Looking at the range, energy and variety of current American fiction, we could say of Fitzgerald's influence on literature what was said of Sir Christopher Wren's influence on London: if it's his monument you want, look around you.

But there are more evident traces of *Gatsby* to be found in modern American fiction, and George Garrett (1985) points to some of these:

> The signs and portents of Joan Didion, for example, or of Renata Adler, are rooted in Fitzgerald's acres of ashes in *Gatsby*, as are the economic minimalism of Raymond Carver, the half-stoned nihilism that pervades the stories of Ann Beattie, the lyrical ambience of the novels and stories of Richard Yates. Gore Vidal, not deeply sympathetic to Fitzgerald, is nevertheless clearly admiring of the 'small but perfect operation' of *Gatsby* (p. 103).

Further detective work on *Gatsby*'s influence has been undertaken by Richard Anderson (1985), who points to explicit mentions of *Gatsby* – and/or Gatsby – in Charles Jackson's *Lost Weekend* (1944), Lois Battle's *Southern Women* (1984), J. D. Salinger's *Catcher in the Rye* (1953), Jack Finney's *Marion's Wall* (1973), Robert B. Parker's *A Savage Place* (1981), and John Irving's *The Hotel New Hampshire* (1981). We might also add here the novel we mentioned in the previous chapter, Ken Kolb's *Getting Straight* (1967), in which there is a scene where the protagonist, Harry, has to attend an oral exam for his Literature MA and reacts with homophobic disgust when one of the examiners suggests that, as Harry puts it, 'Nick Carraway is queer for Jay Gatsby' – 'It was like something you'd find written in a public toilet in a bad neighbourhood' (p. 179). An adapted version of this scene was to become the hilarious climax of the 1970 film of the book which starred Elliot Gould.

Gatsby's presence in British fiction has been less strong and explicit but there is one novel that is worth mentioning in this context, both because of its intrinsic quality and because its similarities to *Gatsby* could easily be overlooked. This is a novel in which there is no Gatsby, and in which the retrospective narrator is looking back from the age of 65 at a decisively traumatic set of experiences which occurred when he was 12 going on 13; but, like Nick, those experiences caused him to withdraw from life. Like Nick, he acts as a pander, if less wittingly, between two lovers divided by class and financial barriers, during a summer of intense heat which seems to melt down the proprieties; like Nick, he is overawed by a powerful male body; like Nick, he is divided, and finally crushed, between realism and idealism; like Nick, his birthday coincides with the climax of the events in which he is involved; and, like Nick, his trauma is deepened by a lethal gunshot. As well as these similarities, there is phrasing that would not be out of place in Fitzgerald's novel: 'I was crossing the rainbow bridge from reality to dream' (p. 77); 'I was in love with the exceptional, and ready to sacrifice all normal happenings to it' (p. 94). The novel in question is *The Go-Between* (1953) and its author was the same person who, 28 years earlier, had dismissed the story of *Gatsby* as absurd: L. P. Hartley. Perhaps his dismissal was proportionate to the effect that Fitzgerald's novel had on him and it may be that elements of it stayed in his subconscious and fed into the making of his most accomplished work.

A less extensive but more evident allusion to *Gatsby* occurs at the beginning of Graham Swift's novel *Waterland* (1983):

'And don't forget,' my father would say, as if he expected me at any moment to up and leave to seek my fortune in the wide world, 'whatever you learn about people, however bad they turn out, each one of them has a heart, and each one of them was once a tiny baby sucking his mother's milk . . .' (p. 1)

The differences between this paternal advice and the paternal advice with which *Gatsby* opens, and the relation of each opening to the text which follows, each of which seeks to understand trauma by turning it into a story, are worth pondering.

Doubtless other traces of *Gatsby*, both explicit and implicit, can be found in English fiction and it is interesting to keep alert for them. Most modern British writers, like most modern American writers, will have read *Gatsby* and have learned from it about style and narrative technique, even if it does not show directly in their work. In the last year of his life, on 20 May 1940, Fitzgerald wrote to Maxwell Perkins asking about the fate of what would become his most famous and enduring novel:

> Would the 25 cent press keep *Gatsby* in the public eye – or *is the book unpopular*. Has it *had* its chance? Would a popular reissue in that series with a preface *not* by me but by one of its admirers – I can maybe pick one – make it a favourite with class rooms, profs, lovers of English prose – anybody. But to die, so completely and unjustly after having given so much. Even now there is little published in American fiction that doesn't slightly have my stamp – in a *small* way I was an original.

The modest adverb and adjective – 'slightly' and 'small' – show the chastened state of the middle-aged man who had once believed that 'life was something you dominated if you were any good'. But even in his reduced circumstances he could see that his work had had its effect on American fiction; he might not have been able to foresee, however, how large and lasting that effect on both American fiction and American culture would be.

STUDY QUESTIONS FOR CHAPTER 5

1. How might you adapt *Gatsby* for the stage today? What scenes and characters would you include, what would you leave out, and what, if anything, might you add?

2. If you had to turn *Gatsby* into a film today, how would you go about the task and what actors would you choose for the key roles? If you are familiar with one or more of the existing *Gatsby* films, explain how your adaptation would compare and contrast with these.

3. *Gatsby* has been made into a successful opera, and it was adapted for a musical at Yale University in 1956, but how would you transform it into a popular musical today which would attract twenty-first-century audiences but preserve the essential qualities of the novel? What would your key songs be, what kinds of lyrics/music would they have, and what kinds of dance routines might you want to include?

CHAPTER 6

GUIDE TO FURTHER READING

EDITIONS OF *THE GREAT GATSBY*

Cambridge edition. Bruccoli, M. J. (ed.), *The Great Gatsby*. (Cambridge: Cambridge University Press, 1991). This critical edition from the world's leading Fitzgerald scholar is an indispensable text to consult for the reader and student who wish to explore *Gatsby* in depth. It includes a chronology of composition and publication, an introduction, a definitive text of the novel, textual and explanatory notes, and appendices on: the short story 'Absolution'; the title; the original dust jacket; the relationship between Fitzgerald's fictional geography and the real geography of Queens and Nassau County on Long Island; and the chronological inconsistencies and difficulties of the novel. A sixth appendix is a manuscript draft of the Gatsby–Tom confrontation scene, and the seventh is Fitzgerald's introduction to the 1934 Modern Library reprint.

Everyman edition. *The Great Gatsby* (London: Everyman's Library, 1991). Especially valuable for its introduction by Malcolm Bradbury, a distinguished critic with a special interest in American literature and a practising novelist with a keen interest both in technique and in the representation of social reality. The introduction succeeds in being both reader-friendly and critically sophisticated. Also includes a helpful bibliography and chronology.

Oxford World's Classics edition. Prigozy, R. (ed.), *The Great Gatsby* (Oxford: Oxford University Press, 1998). An informative and accessible introduction, a sound bibliography, an informed chronology of Fitzgerald's life, a map of Long Island, and helpful notes.

Penguin edition. Introduction and notes by Tanner, T. *The Great Gatsby* (London: Penguin, 2000). Tanner provides not so much an introduction as an original essay, but, given that, the essay is very insightful and wide-ranging – for example, on the relationship between Gatsby and Trimalchio, the fabulously wealthy, hugely vulgar and wildly extravagant party giver in the Latin novel *Satyricon* (*c*.AD 54–68) by Petronius (active first century AD). Useful notes.

EDITION OF THE GALLEY PROOF VERSION OF *THE GREAT GATSBY*

Cambridge edition of *Trimalchio*. West, J. L. W., III, *Trimalchio: An Early Version of 'The Great Gatsby'* (Cambridge: Cambridge University Press, 2000). Like the Cambridge critical edition of *Gatsby* itself, this critical edition of the galley proof version of what finally became *The Great Gatsby* is an indispensable text to consult for the reader and critic who wants to explore *Gatsby* in depth. By reading this text and comparing and contrasting it with the final published version, it is possible to gain unparalleled insights into the ways in which a good novel became a masterpiece. Contains a chronology of composition and publication, an introduction, the text which West has entitled 'Trimalchio', explanatory notes, four illustrations (two of them are of the real figures on whom Fitzgerald based Tom Buchanan and Jordan Baker), and appendices on Maxwell Perkins' letters of criticism to Fitzgerald, on Trimalchio, and on the possibility that the words 'on the threshold, dazzled by the alabaster light' may have been left out of the famous description in Chapter 1 of *Gatsby* of the room in which Daisy and Jordan are sitting.

FACSIMILE OF *GATSBY* MANUSCRIPT

Bruccoli, M. J. (ed.), *F. Scott Fitzgerald's 'The Great Gatsby': A Facsimile of the Manuscript* (Washington, DC: Microcard

Editions Books, 1973). With this facsimile of the manuscript and the edition of *Trimalchio* noted above, the student of *Gatsby* can trace the genesis of the novel and compare and contrast specific passages. Tantalizingly, however, one stage of the process – the typescript which bridged the gap between manuscript and galley proof – is lost.

CONCORDANCE TO *GATSBY*

Crosland, A., *A Concordance to The Great Gatsby* (Detroit, Michigan: Bruccoli Clark/Gale Research, 1975). Although concordances in book form are likely to be replaced in the twenty-first century by searchable electronic versions, this remains very helpful at present to the student of *Gatsby* because it indicates the frequency and location of every word in the novel.

FITZGERALD'S OTHER WORKS (INCLUDES DETAILS OF US AND UK FIRST EDITIONS OF *GATSBY*)

This lists original American and English editions. A variety of paperback editions is currently available.

Novels

This Side of Paradise. New York: Scribner's, 1920; London: Collins, 1922.

The Beautiful and Damned. New York: Scribner's, 1922; London: Collins, 1923.

The Great Gatsby. New York: Scribner's, 1925; London: Chatto and Windus, 1926.

Tender is the Night. New York: Scribner's, 1934; London: Chatto and Windus, 1934.

The Last Tycoon: An Unfinished Novel. Together with The Great Gatsby and selected stories ['May Day', 'The Diamond as Big as the Ritz', 'The Rich Boy', 'Absolution', 'Crazy Sunday'], ed. E. Wilson. New York: Scribner's, 1941; London: Grey Walls Press, 1949.

The Love of the Last Tycoon: A Western, ed. M. J. Bruccoli. Cambridge: Cambridge University Press (1993). A critical edition of the novel which aims to remove the questionable editorial changes of Edmund Wilson (including the title he chose) and to retrieve the text as it existed at Fitzgerald's death. The result is fascinating and the copious secondary material Bruccoli provides is very interesting. This edition gives insights into Fitzgerald's working methods which have implications for the whole of his oeuvre, including *Gatsby*.

Short stories

Fitzgerald wrote 178 short stories in all. While his short fiction is always intrinsically interesting, and illuminating, in one way or another, in relation to his novels, there are four stories that have particular relevance to *Gatsby* – the three stories of the Gatsby group and 'The Rich Boy'.

The Gatsby group

The Gatsby group consists of three short stories which appeared during the genesis of *Gatsby* and seem especially associated with it. The stories are 'Winter Dreams', 'Absolution' and ' "The Sensible Thing" '. These were originally collected in *All the Sad Young Men* and are now available in the Penguin *Collected Short Stories*.

'The Rich Boy'

'The Rich Boy', also originally collected in *All the Sad Young Men*, includes, at the start of its third paragraph, the famous claim that 'the very rich . . . are different from you and me'. 'The Snows of Kilimanjaro' (1936) by Ernest Hemingway contains the equally famous riposte: 'Yes, they have more money.' 'The Rich Boy' is now also available in the Penguin *Collected Short Stories* and in a separate edition with an introduction by the novelist and short-story writer John Updike (born 1932); 'The Snows of Kilimanjaro' is collected in Hemingway's *The First Forty-Nine Stories* (1944).

Short story collections

Flappers and Philosophers. New York: Scribner's, 1920; London: Collins, 1922.

Tales of the Jazz Age. New York: Scribner's, 1922; London: Collins, 1923.

All the Sad Young Men. New York: Scribner's, 1926.

Taps at Reveille. New York: Scribner's, 1935.

The Stories of F. Scott Fitzgerald, ed. M. Cowley. New York: Scribner's, 1951.

Afternoon of an Author: A Selection of Uncollected Stories and Essays. With introduction and notes by A. Mizener. Princeton, New Jersey: Princeton University Library, 1957; New York: Scribner's, 1958; London: Bodley Head, 1958.

The Pat Hobby Stories, ed. A. Gingrich. New York: Scribner's, 1962; Harmondsworth: Penguin, 1967.

The Apprentice Fiction of F. Scott Fitzgerald, ed. J. Kuehl. New Brunswick, New Jersey: Rutgers University Press, 1965.

The Basil and Josephine Stories, eds J. R. Bryer and J. Kuehl. New York: Scribner's, 1973.

Bits of Paradise: 21 Uncollected Stories by F. Scott and Zelda Fitzgerald, eds M. J. Bruccoli and S. F. Smith [Fitzgerald's daughter]. London: Bodley Head, 1973; New York: Scribner's, 1974.

The Price was High: The Last Uncollected Stories of F. Scott Fitzgerald, ed. M. J. Bruccoli. Quartet Books: London, Melbourne, New York: Quartet Books, 1979.

The Short Stories of F. Scott Fitzgerald: A New Collection, ed. M. J. Bruccoli. New York and London: Scribner's, 1989. Contains the Gatsby group stories and 'The Rich Boy'.

The Collected Short Stories of F. Scott Fitzerald. London: Penguin, 2000.

The Rich Boy ('The Rich Boy', 'The Bridal Party', 'The Last of the Belles') with foreword by John Updike. London: Hesperus, 2003.

Essays

The Crack-Up, ed. E. Wilson. New York: New Directions, 1945. Includes 'The Crack-Up' and seven other essays, and an abridged version of Fitzgerald's notebooks, letters to and from Fitzgerald, three critical essays and an obituary poem. For the student of *Gatsby*, the most important material consists of

Fitzgerald's letters of 1925 to Edmund Wilson and John Peale Bishop and three letters on the novel from T. S. Eliot, Gertrude Stein and Edith Wharton.

Letters

The Letters of F. Scott Fitzgerald, ed. A. Turnbull. New York: Scribner's, 1963; London: Bodley Head, 1964.

Dear Scott/Dear Max: The Fitzgerald/Perkins Correspondence, eds J. Kuehl and J. R. Bryer. New York: Scribner's, 1971; London: Cassell, 1973. Especially important and interesting for the student of *Gatsby*, in view of the role Perkins' letters seem to have played in the revision of *Gatsby*.

As Ever, Scott Fitz – Letters between F. Scott Fitzgerald and his Literary Agent Harold Ober, eds M. J. Bruccoli and J. M. Atkinson. Philadelphia and New York: J. B. Lippincott, 1972; London: Woburn Press, 1973.

Corresponence of F. Scott Fitzgerald, eds M. J. Bruccoli and M. M. Duggan, with S. Walker. New York: Random House, 1980.

Notebooks and Ledger

F. Scott Fitzgerald's Ledger: A Facsimile, ed. M. J. Bruccoli. Washington, DC: Bruccoli Clark/NCR Microcard, 1973.

The Notebooks of F. Scott Fitzgerald, ed. M. J. Bruccoli. New York and London: Harcourt Brace Jovanovich/Bruccoli Clark, 1978.

BIOGRAPHIES

The field of Fitzgerald biography is a fraught one because of the intense passions and imaginary identifications that both Scott and Zelda continue to arouse. In particular, recent years have seen something like a state of war between Scottophiles and Zeldaites, and considerable hostility from some scholarly Fitzgerald loyalists towards the ongoing popular interest in the couple. The student of *Gatsby* who wishes to learn more about Fitzgerald's life in order to increase their understanding and appreciation of the novel should tread carefully and remain sceptical of biographical claims unsupported by evidence or of biographical facts unilluminated by insight. Key biographies are:

Bruccoli, M. J., Smith S. F., Ker, J. P., *The Romantic Egoists* (New York: Scribner's, 1974). This is not a standard biography but a richly illustrated large-format record of Fitzgerald's work and life which reproduces many items from his scrapbooks and adds photographs, extracts from the writings of both Scott and Zelda, and relevant biographical details. It is well worth trying to obtain from a library because it does give a vivid sense of the wider culture out of which *Gatsby* emerged and because it does have specific *Gatsby* material of great interest, including clippings of reviews of the novel, play and silent film, and intriguing still photos of scenes from the play and film.

Bruccoli, M. J., *Some Sort of Epic Grandeur: The Life of F. Scott Fitzgerald, with a genealogical afterword by Scottie Fitzgerald Smith* (USA: Harcourt Brace Jovanovich; London: Hodder and Stoughton, revised edition, 1991). An indispensable biography and reference source, valuable for its careful details of Fitzgerald's finances and its faithful transcriptions from his letters, ledgers and notebooks, but sometimes unthinkingly positivist in its approach and not without its own unacknowledged quirks and prejudices.

Le Vot, A., *F. Scott Fitzgerald: A Biography*, trans. William Byron (New York: Doubleday, 1983). Of all the Fitzgerald biographies, this is the one which perhaps achieves the best balance of responsibility to evidence, sympathy for its subject and perceptive literary criticism; Le Vot had already produced an excellent analysis in French of *Gatsby* (see below) and his discussion of the novel in this biography – for example, of its colour symbolism – is a distinguished piece of interpretation in its own right.

Meyers, J., *Scott Fitzgerald* (New York: HarperCollins, 1994; London: Macmillan, 1994). This biography has been strongly criticized by scholarly Fitzgerald loyalists and Scottophiles –

in particular, Meyers' suggestion that Fitzgerald was a foot fetishist has aroused outrage in some quarters – but, provided that the book is treated with the scepticism proper to all biography, it is a lively and accessible account with some stimulating perspectives.

Mizener, A., *The Far Side of Paradise: A Biography of F. Scott Fitzgerald* (Boston: Houghton Mifflin, 1951; London: Eyre and Spottiswoode, 1951; revised edition, New York: Vintage, 1959; London: Heinemann, 1969). The first Fitzgerald biography and a major contribution to the Fitzgerald revival by one of Fitzgerald's pioneering critics; it remains readable and useful. Its discussion of *Gatsby* incorporates Mizener's 'tragic pastoral' interpretation, which is discussed in Chapter 4 of this guide.

Mizener, A., *Scott Fitzgerald and his World* (London: Thames and Hudson, 1972). Especially interesting for its illustrations, which help to give a sense of the wider cultural world out of which *Gatsby* emerged.

Turnbull, A., *Scott Fitzgerald* (New York: Scribner's, 1962; London: The Bodley Head, 1962). The second Fitzgerald biography; like Mizener's, it remains readable and useful. Its author was 11 years old when he first met Fitzgerald, who was a tenant on his family's country place in Baltimore, and his personal recollections of his subject add an evocative extra dimension to his account.

CRITICISM

This section is subdivided to match the chapters and sections in the guide. Where a critical book or essay has been mentioned in Chapter 4, the bibliographical details are provided below, but the entry is not annotated. Where a critical book or essay is included here for the first time, annotation assessing its value and identifying its main topic(s) is supplied.

Language, Style and Form

Doyno, V. A., 'Patterns in *The Great Gatsby*'. *Modern Fiction Studies*, 12 (1966), 415–26. Reprinted in Piper (1970), pp. 160–7; Donaldson (1984), pp. 94–105. Extract and comment in Tredell (1997), pp. 81–93.

Le Vot, A., '*The Great Gatsby*', in B. Poli (ed.) *Francis Scott Fitzgerald*, (Paris: Librairie Armand Colin, 1969), pp. 21–212. Concise and insightful account, in French, which covers genesis, sources, revisions, structure, language, character, themes, critical fortunes and the French translation. The analysis of Fitzgerald's language and style is especially impressive. Some of the analysis is reiterated and developed in Le Vot's biography of Fitzgerald (see 'Biographies' above).

Miller, J. E., Jr., *The Fictional Technique of F. Scott Fitzgerald* (The Hague: Martinus Nijhoff, 1957). Revised edition, under new title: *F. Scott Fitzgerald: His Art and His Technique* (New York: New York University Press, 1964). Extract and comment in Tredell (1997), pp. 65–72.

Reading: Themes

Romanticism

Gunn, G., 'F. Scott Fitzgerald's *Gatsby* and the imagination of wonder', *Journal of the American Academy of Religion*, 41 (June 1973), 171–83. Contends that the theme of *Gatsby* is 'the energy and quality of the imagination which propels both Gatsby *and* his vision, and which endures, if at all, only in the narrative strategies of Fitzgerald's art'. Reprinted in Donaldson (1984), pp. 228–42 – this quote is from p. 230.

McCall, D., 'The self-same song that found a path': Keats and *The Great Gatsby*, *American Literature*, 42 (1970–1), 521–30. Argues that the influence of Keats on *Gatsby* 'should not be understood exclusively in the terms of "literary imitation"' but that the 'distinguishing and complicated similarity is in a realization of the ambivalence of beauty'; the 'romantic desire for mystical union with the beautiful drives both Keats and Fitzgerald back into legends of "vast obscurity", visionary dreams and loves surrendered to time' (pp. 521–2, 530).

Mizener, A., 'F. Scott Fitzgerald 1896–1940: The Poet of

Borrowed Time', in *Lives of Eighteen from Princeton* (Princeton: Princeton University Press, 1946). Reprinted in Kazin (1962), pp. 23–45. Extract and comment in Tredell (1997), pp. 45–9.

Troy, W., 'Scott Fitzgerald – the authority of failure', *Accent*, 6 (Autumn 1945), 56–60. Reprinted in Hoffman (1962), pp. 224–31; Kazin (1962), pp. 188–94; Mizener (1963), pp. 20–4. Extract and comment in Tredell (1997), pp. 43–5.

America: Dream and History

Barbour, B. M., '*The Great Gatsby* and the American Past', *The Southern Review*, 9 (Spring 1973), 288–99. Complicates and enriches the 'American Dream' interpretation of *Gatsby* by arguing that the novel 'dramatizes the conflict between the two American dreams' – a materialist one, articulated by Benjamin Franklin (1706–90) and a mystical one, articulated by Ralph Waldo Emerson (1803–82) (p. 298).

Bewley, M., 'Scott Fitzgerald's criticism of America'. *Sewanee Review*, 62 (Spring 1954), 223–46. Reprinted in Hoffmann (1962), pp. 263–85; Lockridge (1968), pp. 37–53; Bloom (1986), pp. 11–27. Extract and comment in Tredell (1997), pp. 57–61.

Bicknell, J. W., 'The Waste Land of F. Scott Fitzgerald'. *Virginia Quarterly Review*, 30 (Autumn 1954), 556–72. Reprinted in Eble (1973), pp. 67–80. Comment in Tredell (1997), p. 61.

Callahan, J. F., *The Illusions of a Nation: Myth and History in the Novels of F. Scott Fitzgerald* (Urbana: University of Illinois Press, 1972). Extract and comment in Tredell (1997), pp. 107–11.

Fussell, E. S., 'Fitzgerald's Brave New World'. *ELH: A Journal of English Literary History*, 19: 4 (December 1952), 291–306. Reprinted in revised form in Hoffman (1962), pp. 244–62; Mizener (1963), pp. 43–56. Comment in Tredell (1997), pp. 56–7.

Moyer, K. W., '*The Great Gatsby*: Fitzgerald's meditation on American history', *Fitzgerald/Hemingway Annual 1972* (Washington, DC: NCR Microcard Editions, 1973), 43–57. Argues that *Gatsby* is characterized by a circularity of form (it starts at the end, moves back to the beginning and comes back to the end) and a series of circular movements (e.g. from West to East to West) which reiterate 'the novel's perspective upon American history' as circular. Reprinted in Donaldson (1984), pp. 215–28 – this quote is from p. 217.

Slater, P. G., 'Ethnicity in *The Great Gatsby*', *Twentieth Century Literature*, 19 (1973), pp. 53–62. Extract and comment in Tredell (1997), pp. 111–12.

Stern, M. R., *The Golden Moment: The Novels of F. Scott Fitzgerald* (Urbana: University of Illinois Press, 1970).

Trilling, L., 'F. Scott Fitzgerald', in *The Liberal Imagination: Essays on Literature and Society* (London: Secker and Warburg, 1951), pp. 243–54. Reprinted in Hoffman (1962), pp. 232–43; Kazin (1962), pp. 195–205; Mizener (1963), pp. 11–19; Donaldson (1984), pp. 13–20. Extract and comment in Tredell (1997), pp. 51–6.

America: The 1920s

Berman, R., '*The Great Gatsby' and Modern Times* (Urbana: University of Illinois Press, 1994). Extract and comment in Tredell (1997), pp. 151–7.

—— '*The Great Gatsby* and the twenties', in, R. Prigozy (ed.) *The Cambridge Companion to F. Scott Fitzgerald* (Cambridge: Cambridge University Press, 2002), pp. 79–94.

Forrey, K. 'Negroes in the fiction of F. Scott Fitzgerald'. *Phylon: The Atalanta University Review of Race and Culture*, 48 (1967), 293–8. Extract and comment in Tredell (1997), pp. 93–4.

Goldhurst, W., 'Literary anti-semitism in the 20's'. *American Jewish Congress Bi-Weekly*, 29 (24 December 1962), 10–12.

—— *F. Scott Fitzgerald and his contemporaries* (Cleveland: Cleveland World Publishing, 1963) pp. 176–87.

Hindus, M., 'F. Scott Fitzgerald and literary anti-semitism: a footnote on the mind of the 20's'. *Commentary*, 3 (June 1947), 508–16.

Kopf, J. Z., 'Meyer Wolfshiem and Robert Cohn: a study of Jewish type and stereotype'. *Tradition*, 10 (Spring 1969), 93–104.

Lhamon, W. T., Jr., 'The Essential Houses of *The Great Gatsby*'.

Markham Review, 6 (Spring 1977), 56–60. Argues that the different 'houses' in *Gatsby* – the Buchanan mansion, Gatsby's mansion and Myrtle's apartment – are essential structurally and thematically to the novel's representation of modern America: each of the three houses represents a different social group but all three groups subscribe across social divisions to the same unsatisfying, destructive set of values. Reprinted in Donaldson (1984), pp. 166–75.

Westbrook, J. S., 'Nature and Optics in *The Great Gatsby*'. *American Literature*, 32 (March 1960), 79–84. Extract and comment in Tredell (1997), pp. 74–80.

Money

Friedrich, O., 'F. Scott Fitzgerald: Money, money, money', *American Scholar*, 29 (Summer 1960), 392–405. Interesting though critically unsophisticated essay which uses impressionistic biography and sociology to argue that Nick's final judgement on the Buchanans is 'an explosion of hatred against all the things [Fitzgerald] had once admired' – the things that supposedly made the very rich 'different' – and that this judgement extends, at the end of the novel, 'through Gatsby's passionate illusion to the national illusion' (p. 399).

Godden, R., '*The Great Gatsby*: Glamour on the turn'. *Journal of American Studies*, 16:3 (1982), 343–71. Collected in Godden, *Fictions of capital: The American novel from James to Mailer* (Cambridge: Cambridge University Press, 1990), pp. 78–203. Extract and comment in Tredell (1997), pp. 137–41. Also discussed in Tanner's introduction to Penguin edition of *Gatsby*.

Hemingway, E., 'The Snows of Kilimanjaro' in *The First Forty-Nine Stories* (London: Arrow Books, Random House, 2004).

Lewis, R., 'Money, love, and aspiration in *The Great Gatsby*', in Bruccoli (1985), pp. 41–57. Argues that the 'unique contribution' of *Gatsby* is 'the identification' of money and love – the 'acquisition of money and love are both part of the same dream, the will to return to the quintessential unity that exists only at birth and at death' (p. 56).

Shrubb, E. P., 'The girls and the money: reflections on *The Great*

Gatsby'. Sydney Studies in English 11 (1985), 95–102. Provides an interesting and lively if sometimes sketchy contrast to the 'return to the tomb/womb' interpretation which Lewis offers or the 'pessimism' reading of Bicknell. Stresses the hopefulness and forward thrust of the novel in which fighting towards the future is at least a way of getting a past: 'what the tale tells us [presumably men] at its end, as so often throughout, is to row like hell after the girls and the money' (p. 102).

Sexuality and Gender

Corrigan, R. A., 'Somewhere West of Laramie, on the road to West Egg: automobiles, fillies, and the West in *The Great Gatsby'. Journal of Popular Culture*, 7 (1973), 152–8. According to Corrigan, Jordan Baker's name is a compound of the brand names of two cars: the Baker Electric, which appeared around the turn of the century but did not survive long (but see entry for MacPhee below), and the Jordan, a widely advertised car of the 1920s. Corrigan offers a very interesting exploration of the ads for different Jordan car models of the period and links them with the characterization of Jordan Baker. For example, one ad claimed the Jordan car had 'a savor of [golf] links about it' (p. 156), and in *Gatsby* Nick associates Jordan with golf links on two occasions (pp. 57, 161), while another, aimed at women drivers, said the Jordan Playboy was built for 'a bronco-busting, steer-roping girl' who lived '[s]omewhere West of Laramie' (p. 154). Jordan Baker is not as far west as this reincarnation of Calamity Jane for the auto age, but she does come originally from the Midwest, and she is an active and successful sportswoman on the links if not in the rodeo.

Fraser, K., 'Another reading of *The Great Gatsby'. English Studies in Canada*, 5 (Autumn 1979), 330–43. Reprinted in Bloom (1986), pp. 57–70; Donaldson (1984), pp. 140–53. Discussion and extract in Tredell (1997), pp. 130–5. See also Wasiolek below.

Fryer, S. B., *Fitzgerald's new women: harbingers of change* (Ann Arbor: UMI Research Press, 1988). Comment in Tredell (1997), p. 137.

Korenman, J. S., ' "Only her hairdresser . . . ": another look at Daisy Buchanan'. *American Literature*, 46 (January 1974), 574–8. Extract and comment in Tredell (1997), pp. 112–15.

MacPhee, L. E., '*The Great Gatsby*'s "romance of motoring": Nick Carraway and Jordan Baker'. *Modern Fiction Studies*, 18 (Summer 1972), 207–12. Like Corrigan (see above), MacPhee associates Jordan Baker's forename with Jordan cars, but contends that her surname alludes to Baker 'Fastex' Velvet, made by A. T. Baker, a company which, like Jordan cars, ran a series of ads in the 1920s, one of which claimed that 'the natural human craving for luxury is more than satisfied by the beauty and soft touch of Baker velours and velvets. On your furniture – Baker cut velour. In your motor car – Baker Fastex Velvet' (p. 211). MacPhee's overall argument is that Nick, in throwing over the girl whose name spells automobiles, 'also repudiates very pointedly what the automobile has represented in the book . . . the restless and potentially destructive impulses of our culture' (pp. 207, 212).

Person, L. S., Jr., ' "Herstory" and Daisy Buchanan', *American Literature*, 50 (May 1978), 250–7. Extract and comment in Tredell (1997), pp. 116–22.

Wasiolek, E., 'The sexual drama of Nick and Gatsby'. *The International Fiction Review*, 19 (1992), 14–22. Argues provocatively that Nick's support for Gatsby confronts us 'with the sympathy of one homosexual for another' and accuses Fraser (see above), despite his 'excellent perceptions', of ignoring 'the central issues of the novel' – 'Nick and Gatsby's relationship and Gatsby and Daisy's love' – and of being 'too timid . . . in making firm and definite Nick's homosexual proclivities' by his refusal to read the Nick/McKee scene as a definitely gay one (pp. 18, 19).

Appearance and Reality

Berman, R., '*The Great Gatsby' and Fitzgerald's world of ideas* (Tuscaloosa: University of Alabama Press, 1997).

Dessner, L. J., 'Photography and *The Great Gatsby*'. *Essays in Literature*, 6 (1979), 79–89. Points out that *Gatsby* 'surveys and evaluates many uses of photography' and that photography,

because it is 'a mode of perception', 'carries implicit philo-
sophic assumptions' – it 'is a way people . . . reinforce their
assumptions about the nature of reality and time'. Also in
Donaldson (1984), pp. 175–86 – this quote is from p. 175.

Lockridge, E., 'F. Scott Fitzgerald's *trompe l'oeil* and *The Great
Gatsby*'s buried plot'. *Journal of Narrative Technique*, 17:2
(1987), 163–83. An ingenious interpretation which finds a con-
cealed thriller/detective story plot in *Gatsby* that ultimately
has philosophical implications. According to Lockridge,
Fitzgerald's technique reveals Nick as an unreliable narrator
whose 'own "testimony" resembles that of a Doctor Watson
[in the Sherlock Holmes stories], deftly managing whenever
humanly possible to miss the point'. As there is no equivalent
of Holmes in the text, Lockridge steps into the role, and makes
intriguing suggestions about the deaths of Myrtle and Gatsby.
Myrtle's death, he claims, is murder; Daisy is aware of who
Myrtle is, deliberately uses her relationship with Gatsby to
make Tom jealous and try to save her marriage, and seizes the
chance to kill Myrtle when she runs in front of the car.
Gatsby's death is also murder, but Wilson may not be the killer.
An alternative scenario is that Wolfshiem wants Gatsby out of
the way because he has outlived his usefulness and become
unreliable due to his obsession with Daisy; he therefore orders
his henchmen, who are already installed in Gatsby's mansion,
to bump him off, and just after they have done so, Wilson
arrives – and can conveniently be killed as well and take the rap
for Gatsby's murder. Lockridge acknowledges that this is speculative, that there is no way to be sure of what did happen, but
sees this uncertainty as an example of a process evident
throughout *Gatsby*: 'the closer the gaze and the sharper the
focus, the greater the mystery flowering in the place of seeming
certainty, as though the entire novel were a masterly *trompe
l'oeil* [an illusion that deceives the eye]'. In this way, the novel
'embodies a modern predicament', an existential and philosophical predicament: 'the belief that it is impossible to see or
know anything absolutely' (pp. 178–9).

Stallman, R. W., 'Gatsby and the hole in time'. *Modern Fiction
Studies*, 1:4 (November 1955), 2–16. Reprinted in Stallman,

The Houses that James Built and Other Literary Studies (Michigan: Michigan State University Press, 1961), pp. 150–7. Extract and comment in Tredell (1997), pp. 61–5.
White, P., *Gatsby's Party: The System and the List in Contemporary Narrative* (West Lafayette, Indiana: Purdue University Press, 1992). Extract and comment in Tredell (1997), pp. 145–50.

Critical Reception and Publishing History
Bloom, H. (ed.), *Modern Critical Interpretations of 'The Great Gatsby'* (New York: Chelsea House, 1986).
Bruccoli, M. J. (ed.), *New Essays on 'The Great Gatsby'* (Cambridge: Cambridge University Press, 1985).
Bryer, J. R. (ed.), *F. Scott Fitzgerald: The Critical Reception* (New York: Butt Franklin, 1978).
Donaldson, S. (ed.), *Critical Essays on F. Scott Fitzgerald's 'The Great Gatsby'* (Boston: G. K. Hall, 1984).
Eble, K. (ed.), *Scott Fitzgerald: a Collection of Criticism* (New York: McGraw-Hill, 1973).
Hoffman, F. J. (ed.), *'The Great Gatsby': A Study* (New York: Scribner's, 1962).
Kazin, A. (ed.), *F. Scott Fitzgerald: The Man and his Work* (New York: Collier, 1962).
Lockridge, E. H. (ed.), *Twentieth Century Interpretations of 'The Great Gatsby'* (Englewood Cliffs, New Jersey: Prentice-Hall, 1968).
Mizener, A. (ed.), *Scott Fitzgerald: A Collection of Critical Essays* (Englewood Cliffs, New Jersey: Prentice-Hall, 1963).
Piper, H. D. (ed.), *Fitzgerald's 'The Great Gatsby': The Novel, The Critics, The Background* (New York: Scribner's, 1970).
Tredell, N. (ed.), *F. Scott Fitzgerald: 'The Great Gatsby': A Reader's Guide to Essential Criticism* (London and Basingstoke: Palgrave Macmillan, 1997).

Adaptation, interpretation and influence
Play and/or film adaptations: books and essays
Dixon, W. W., *The Cinematic Vision of F. Scott Fitzgerald* (Ann Arbor, Michigan: UMI Research Press, 1986), pp. 20–32.

—— 'The Three Film Versions of *The Great Gatsby*: A Vision Deferred'. *Literature Film Quarterly*, 31:4 (2004), 287–94.

Margolies, A., 'Novel to Play to Film: Four Versions of *The Great Gatsby*', in Donaldson (1984), pp. 187–200.

Morsberger, R., 'Trimalchio in West Egg: *The Great Gatsby* Onstage'. *Prospects: An Annual Journal of American Cultural Studies*, 5 (1980), 489–506.

Phillips, G. (S. J.) *Fiction, Film and F. Scott Fitzgerald* (Chicago: Loyola University Press, 1986), pp. 101–24.

DVDs

DVDs of the 1974 and 2000 TV film are available, but a DVD or video version of the 1949 film has been difficult to obtain for some time. It is to be hoped that a DVD version can be brought out soon.

The Great Gatsby (1974). Paramount Home Entertainment. 135 mins.

The Great Gatsby (2000), with Scott Fitzgerald episode of A & E's Biography. A & E Home Video. 100 mins.

Opera

www.schirmer.com/composers/harbison_gatsby.html

Literature

Anderson, R., 'Gatsby's Long Shadow: Influence and Endurance', in Bruccoli (1985), pp. 15–40.

Garrett, G., 'Fire and Freshness: A Matter of Style in *The Great Gatsby*', in Bruccoli (1985), pp. 101–16.

Hartley, L. P., *The Go-Between* (Harmondsworth: Penguin, 1975).

Kolb, K., *Getting Straight* (London: Barrie and Rockliff, 1968).

Swift, G., *Waterland* (London: Picador, 1984).

INDEX

The Great Gatsby has an entry of its own. Fitzgerald's other works are indexed under his surname.